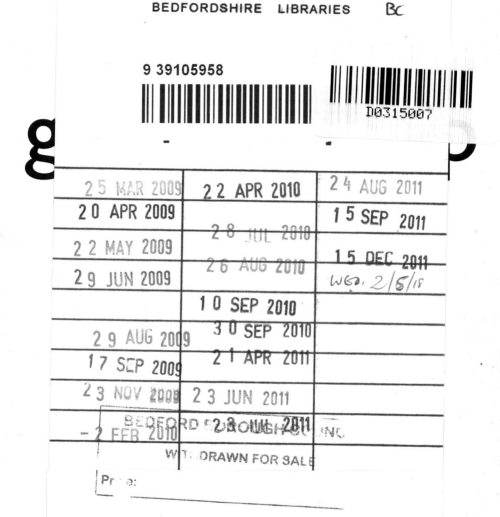

A Pyramid Sport Paperback

hamlyn

Lower your
golf handicap

Nick Wright

CONTENTS

An Hachette Livre UK Company
www.hachettelivre.co.uk

A Pyramid Paperback

First published in Great Britain in 2006 by Hamlyn,
a division of Octopus Publishing Group Ltd
2–4 Heron Quays, London E14 4JP
www.octopusbooks.co.uk

This edition published in 2009

Copyright © Octopus Publishing Group Limited 2006, 2009

Distributed in the U.S. and Canada by Octopus Books USA:
c/o Hachette Book Group USA
237 Park Avenue
New York NY 10017

This material was previously published as *Lower Your Golf Handicap*

ISBN: 978-0-600-61883-6

A CIP catalogue record for this book is available from the
British Library

Printed and bound in China

10 9 8 7 6 5 4 3 2 1

There is no doubt that golf tuition has progressed in leaps and bounds over the course of the last decade. Coaching methods have improved, theories among the leading teachers have become more standardized, and high-speed video analysis has taken the guesswork out of the learning process by enabling you to scrutinize your technique down to the tiniest detail. There has also never been a greater choice of instructional information available for golfers. You can now find a wealth of educational material in books, magazine articles, web sites, videos, CD-ROMs and DVDs.

With all this material at our fingertips, and with golf club manufacturers producing increasingly forgiving clubs and aerodynamic balls, one could easily be forgiven for assuming that the handicap of the average club golfer must be spiralling downwards at a remarkable rate of knots, and that it is surely only a matter of time before we are all playing off scratch, breaking course records and registering to play in the Masters or the US Open. Unfortunately, this has not been the case. In fact, the average club golfer's handicap has remained virtually unchanged – at around 24 for men and 36 for ladies – for at least the past decade.

So why is it that the vast majority of golfers do not ever seem to improve their golf? The main reason is because very few golfers are actually committed and disciplined enough to go out and work on their game on a regular basis. Taking lessons and reading books is all well and good, but if you do not spend enough time beating balls on the range and practising your chipping and putting, you will never be able to turn the theory into reality. At the same time, there are also plenty of golfers who spend many hours of their spare time practising, yet still fail to achieve

a significant fall in handicap. Why? The answer is usually because they do not practise effectively or with any structured purpose.

The aim of this book is to provide you with all the information you need to make a significant reduction in your handicap within just ten weeks. In addition to improving your attitude, mental approach, course management and technique in all of the key areas of the game, you will have a dedicated 10-week plan to follow so that you can build and develop your skills in the most time-effective manner. As you follow the plan, you will also constantly be able to highlight and target the key weaknesses that consistently destroy your scores.

The purpose of this book is not to create the perfect swing. The biggest mistake to avoid before you start flicking through these pages is to assume that you will need to give your swing a Nick Faldo-style overhaul in order to become a much better player. That is not the case. Although there will be plenty of pointers on swing theory and the technicalities of the game throughout the book, I will constantly remind you that you do not need a flawless technique in order to become a single-figure golfer. You simply need to become proficient in most areas of the game – particularly around the greens. And that is well within the reach of most club golfers.

Good luck and enjoy the book.
Nick Wright

Your very first step to becoming a single-figure golfer within the next ten weeks is making the commitment to devote time to working on your game. Without the correct attitude, the determination and desire to really improve your golf dramatically, you will inevitably stumble at the very first hurdle during the plan. This very first step is the most important of the whole programme.

Throughout this first section of the book, you will be continually reminded that you do not need to play flawless golf in order to become a single-figure golfer.

In this section you will learn how to set yourself realistic and achievable goals, and methods to boost your confidence, concentration and self-belief.

You will also learn how to select the best equipment for your individual game and some of the basic course management and practice techniques that will enable you to maximize your potential on the course and your work on the range away from it.

The skills you need to become a single-figure golfer

One of the greatest misconceptions among higher handicap golfers and beginners is that there is some mystical swing secret that must be learned to become an accomplished golfer. These same golfers also believe that single-figure players have smooth, free-flowing swings, flawless techniques and that they strike the ball perfectly, right out of the middle of the sweet spot on the clubface, every single time. Obviously, none of these is true.

The good news is that, in most cases, a 9-handicapper is no better than average in most areas of the game. Contrary to what you may have thought, to become a single-figure golfer you do not need to be able to carry the ball 250 yards-plus through the air off the tee, you do not need to strike every iron shot purely and you do not need to be a magician around the greens and hole every putt you look at.

Most golfers have the physical ability to play good golf. What usually prevents them from fulfilling their potential is insufficient self-belief, a lack of desire, an unwillingness to take lessons and to practise the skills learned, poor course management or simply not enough play. Single-figure players can appear in many different guises. Some are poor drivers and long-iron players who save their scores by chipping and putting for pars and bogeys. Other golfers are long and straight off the tee yet cannot fully capitalize on their distance because they are poor iron players and lack confidence on the greens. Older and more experienced players often maintain a low handicap simply by playing to their strengths, keeping the ball in play and not taking unnecessary risks.

You do not have to master any particular part of the game to reach single figures, nor do you have to be hugely talented. Think about how many times you three-putted during your last round of golf. You will immediately find three or four wasted strokes there. Now think about how many times you dropped shots through making the wrong decisions or you made a bogey or worse by under-clubbing.

Add the total together, and you will discover that, invariably, you are wasting around eight or nine shots per round. Eliminate those straight away and you are already halfway to playing off single figures.

CONFIDENCE

The importance of a positive state of mind There is no greater commodity on the golf course than confidence. When everything is going well and you are in control of your game, you feel that there is nothing you cannot achieve.

Unfortunately, these days are rarities for most amateur golfers.

One of the keys to playing good golf is to get yourself into this confident frame of mind more often.

PATIENCE

The ability to grind out a score Television commentators talk about a player 'grinding out a score'. The player is not on top of his or her game and is struggling to make things happen, but is still managing to compile a decent score – normally by making a lot of safe pars without threatening the hole for birdies.

The top professionals can turn a potentially mediocre round of 74 into a 70 simply by remaining cool and waiting for the right opportunity to present itself. At your own level, the ability to turn an 85 into an 80 is invaluable. Simply thinking sensibly will save you many strokes throughout the year.

AWARENESS

Watch and learn The best golfers are very observant on the golf course, from monitoring the strength and direction of the wind to checking out the positioning of hazards and potential danger areas.

Always watch how your playing partners' shots behave once they land on the fairway or green so that you have as much information at your disposal as possible before you play each shot.

DISCIPLINE

Resist the score-wrecking temptations
Self-discipline is one of your greatest allies on the golf course. Most golfers waste countless strokes through poor decision-making and through attempting to play over-ambitious recovery shots. Know your limitations as a golfer and never attempt shots that you know you cannot play.

SELF-BELIEF

If you do not have faith in your ability, nobody will You will always struggle to become a single-figure golfer if you do not believe you are capable of becoming one. How many times have you posted a good round for 14 or 15 holes, then totted up your scorecard and discovered that if you could just play the remaining four holes in 4-over par, you would break 100, 90 or 80? Then what happens? Your game goes to pieces, you lose your focus and confidence and you end up ruining your score completely.

Avoid setting yourself limitations as that will impede your progress. Always go for the best score possible rather than aiming for certain targets, such as 90 or 80.

CONCENTRATION

Think before you play Concentration does not necessarily mean that you must become so wrapped up in your own thoughts on the golf course that you do not say a word to anyone during the round. It simply means that you should be focused when preparing for and playing each and every shot.

In between, you can do as you like, as long as you don't lose your rhythm, but when it comes to the business of hitting the ball, concentrate on that alone.

Your first step: set yourself achievable goals

Goals are a crucial part of improving your game. Obviously, without a clear idea of what you actually want to achieve, it is very unlikely that you will ever achieve it. The more detailed your target is, the more real it becomes and the more your brain will focus its efforts to achieve it. In order for your goals to be effective, they must fulfil the following criteria:

SPECIFIC

The more specific a goal the better. In this case it is simple. Your goal is to have a handicap of 9.4 within ten weeks of committing to the game-improvement plan.

MEASURABLE

All goals must be measurable. In your case, your scores in both competitions and social rounds of golf will enable you to chart your level of performance and progress on a regular basis.

ACHIEVABLE

This is the most difficult element of the goal-setting process. A goal that is too easy to achieve is worthless. Likewise, setting yourself a goal of achieving a plus-1 handicap in ten weeks if you are currently a 28-handicapper is also unrealistic. Set a target that will stretch your capabilities but which is still achievable.

REALISTIC

For any goal to be achievable it must also be realistic. For a beginner to reach single figures in just ten weeks is asking a lot, but a mid- to high-handicap golfer should be capable of lowering his or her score by seven or eight shots within this period of time.

TIME

For a goal to be effective, it must have a time limit. Once again, this is simple to monitor. Your target is to achieve your new, lower handicap within the ten-week time frame recommended in this book.

You can remember these goals by thinking of them as SMART
- **S**pecific
- **M**easurable
- **A**chievable
- **R**ealistic
- **T**ime

Adopt a positive approach to your golf

Fairway bunkers, intimidating water carries, fast greens and narrow fairways are all challenges that have to be faced, and overcome, at some time, but on the golf course you are usually your own greatest adversary. How many times have you talked yourself into topping drives, fluffing chip shots and missing short putts? How many times have you stood on the first tee thinking about everything that can possibly go wrong rather than what could go right? The first step in your journey towards single-figure golf is to stop that negative self-talk straight away. It serves no purpose other than to destroy your confidence.

THINK OF YOURSELF AS A SINGLE-FIGURE GOLFER – NOW!

After you have set your goals for the next few months and beyond, what is the first step that you need to make on your route to becoming a single-figure golfer? Believe in your own technique, know your own game and take a positive attitude onto the golf course every time you play.

There is a phrase in psychology: 'As you think, you become.' Start thinking of yourself as a single-figure player – imagine what it would be like, how you would think on the course, how you would approach the game and how confident you would be if you were a single-figure player.

AVOIDING COSTLY MENTAL ERRORS

Everybody makes mistakes in golf. While physical mistakes are acceptable and to be expected in golf, mental mistakes through poor decision-making are totally avoidable. You can stop the rot right now and make huge improvements to this crucial part of

the game almost instantly. Cast your mind back to your last round of golf and add up all the wasted shots you made. It is very likely that while a poor shot is often to blame for making a bogey or worse, the cause for such a shot was a mental error. Think constructively about every single shot you play. Plan ahead and weigh up all the different scenarios in your mind before you commit to a shot. Constantly ask yourself: 'Is this the best way to play this shot?' If

after all your planning and preparation you still hit a bad shot, that is golf, but at least you have done all you possibly can to prepare professionally.

OVERCOME YOUR FEAR OF FAILURE

The single biggest factor preventing amateur golfers from playing to their full potential is the fear of failure. Ask yourself this simple question: 'Why is it that I can confidently hit the ball perfectly on the range with an uninhibited and free-flowing swing, then stand on the first tee in a club competition the following day a nervous wreck and barely be able to move the club away from the ball?' Is it because you have become a bad player overnight or because your swing has suddenly developed a destructive swing flaw? Of course not. The difference is that on the range you have no fear of failure. You cannot lose your ball, you cannot make double or triple bogeys and there are no harsh consequences such as penalty shots for your wayward shots; you simply tee up another ball and try again.

Your ultimate goal is to take that fearless approach out onto the golf course. Your first step is to make a commitment to never make a half-hearted or tentative swing again. Make a pact with yourself to swing positively every time and to play each shot the way you want to play it. This is a difficult attitude to take straight into a competitive round or even a social game among friends, so it is a good idea to play nine holes by yourself when you do not have the added pressure of worrying about how your new mental approach will work in front of your peers.

Of course, you will not strike the ball perfectly every time. You will still hit wayward shots, mistime the ball every now and then, and find yourself in the trees occasionally, too, but it certainly will not be any more than normal. In fact, committing 100 per cent to each and every shot will enable you to keep the ball in play more easily than if you try to steer the ball down the fairway. You will also feel much more relaxed knowing that you are playing the game the way you want to play rather than spending four hours on the golf course thinking about what you do not want to do and worrying about the consequences.

REMEMBER THAT ALL HOLES ARE IMPORTANT, NOT JUST THE FIRST FEW
One of the biggest problems for golfers of any level – even the top professionals – is recovering from a poor start to the round. Almost every golfer stands on the first tee with high expectations of how they are going to play and it is difficult not to get angry or dejected when, after building up your hopes, you make a double bogey or worse at the very first hole. However, you should remember that many top players have gone on to post course records and win tournaments after some highly inauspicious starts.

Take Tiger Woods in the 1997 Masters, for example. After nine holes of the first round he stood on the 10th tee at 4-over par and seemingly on his way to an unimpressive score and possible elimination from the tournament. Rather than getting down on himself and allowing negativity to get the better of him, Woods went on to produce a barrage of birdies and played near perfect golf during the remaining 63 holes of the tournament. He finished a record 12 strokes clear of his nearest competitor and his 18-under par winning total was also a championship low score. That just goes to show you that all 18 holes are important in a round of golf, not just the first few.

HOW TO STRENGTHEN YOUR MENTAL GAME

Visualize each shot in your mind's eye before you play it. Picture yourself making the perfect swing and the perfect contact with the ball. Picture the flight and trajectory of the shot you want to hit and see the ball land close to your intended target. Keep this image in your mind as you play the shot and make the picture as vivid as possible so that it becomes more realistic. You can do this at home or on the course itself.

Select small targets to aim at

Top professionals never hit a shot without having a target to aim at and nor should you. A target gives your brain a task to focus on. Simply aiming somewhere down the fairway or on the green is not specific enough and will inevitably lead to sloppy play. Pick out a small target, such as a bush in the distance or a particular quarter of the green. This policy makes you much more task-orientated, improves your concentration and increases your margin for error.

Golf is not just about the quality of your good shots. It is the quality of your misses and bad shots that determines how well you score.

Commit 100 per cent to every shot

One of the most significant differences between a professional golfer and an amateur is that after playing a poor shot, the professional will stand over the ball the next time and commit fully to the shot, while the amateur is likely to allow the first shot to affect his or her confidence. Full commitment is one of the secrets to good golf. Swinging half-heartedly and nervously increases your chances of hitting a poor shot, so make sure that you commit fully every time.

Focus on what you want to do

How many times have you stood over the ball and said to yourself: 'I do not want to hit it in the water,' 'I do not want to go in the bunker,' or 'I do not want to top this drive' and then proceeded to do exactly that?

Change your internal dialogue so that, in future, you tell yourself what you want to do rather than what you do not want to do.

Focus on the shot, not the swing

One of the biggest mistakes you can make is to assume that if you have hit a good shot you must have made a good swing. That is not always true. It is possible to hit good shots with bad swings and terrible shots with perfect swings. From now on, think about the shot you want to hit, not the swing you want to make. The former will automatically improve the latter.

Be aware of hazards, but do not focus on them

Hazards, such as bunkers, trees, water and rough, are integral parts of the golf course, and it would be foolish to recommend that you should ignore them when planning a shot. Tiger Woods

says that he is always aware of the positioning of hazards, but once he has used that information to help him select his club and strategy, he then forgets about them completely and concentrates on the shot he wants to play. You should take this approach as well.

Never dwell on your bad shots during a round

It is very difficult not to become annoyed or frustrated after a particularly bad hole, but dwelling on your mistakes can make things even worse.

Instead of focusing on the bad shots that you have played during a round of golf, think instead about the good ones. This goes for your post-round analysis, too. We all like to sit down at the end of the round with our playing partners and reminisce over what might have been if, say, we had not three-putted the fifth hole, fluffed that chip on the 15th or driven out of bounds at the last. Rather than paying attention to what you did poorly, focus on what you did well. Replay the good shots over and over in your mind.

Building a library of positive memories will give you a resource to dip into whenever you feel nervous or anxious about playing a shot, and the confidence to strike positively.

Review your equipment

One aspect of the game that amateurs pay scant attention to is the suitability of their equipment. Most golfers purchase 'standard' clubs straight off the shelf, very often after seeing an advert on television or in a golf magazine that has convinced them that a particular manufacturer's latest wonder clubs will transform their game overnight. In many cases, these golfers do not even try the clubs before they walk out of the store.

Invest in a new set of golf clubs if you wish, but always hit some practice balls with a selection of similar-style clubs before you make your final decision and ask the retailer to custom-fit the clubs to your individual physique and swing. Most pro shops and specialist golf stores include fitting as a free part of their service.

WHY YOU SHOULD USE CUSTOM-FITTED GOLF CLUBS

It is amazing how many amateur golfers play with clubs that do not suit the characteristics of their swing or their physique.

By varying the length and flex of the shaft and the lie angle of the clubhead, golf clubs can be adjusted to suit players of different heights, physiques and swing speeds. You can even adjust your clubs so that they will counteract your slice or hook.

You will never reach your full potential if you play with clubs that have not been correctly fitted to match your individual swing style, height and build. You may be able to hit with these clubs perfectly well most of the time, because you will instinctively adapt

yourself to whatever clubs you may have, but it is far better to match the clubs to your swing rather than the other way round.

HOW TO GET YOUR CLUBS ADJUSTED OR MADE TO MEASURE

The benefits of custom club-fitting are recognized by pro shops and specialist golf stores, most of whom incorporate a fitting procedure into the standard customer service free of charge. However, you can always have your existing set of clubs upgraded or adjusted. A specialist club-fitter will analyze your swing and physique and then tweak your existing set to match your ideal specifications simply by altering the lie of the clubhead and fitting new shafts and/or grips. This is a cost-effective alternative to spending a lot of money on brand new clubs, particularly if you have grown attached to your current set.

INVEST IN YOUR WEDGES

Over two-thirds of the shots you play during a round of golf will be struck from within 60 or 70 yards from the green – prime wedge territory. Most of the world's top golfers carry at least three wedges – a lob wedge, sand wedge and pitching wedge – in their bag.

Adding a lob wedge to your set is advisable. Most amateur golfers will need to use a wedge regularly during the course of a round, but they will rarely use a 2-iron or 3-iron. Consider leaving out one of the longer irons that you do not hit that often in favour of a specialist wedge. Your short game will improve dramatically.

DO NOT NEGLECT OR FORGET YOUR PUTTER

You will use your putter almost twice as much during a round as your driver, so it makes sense to invest a little extra time and, possibly, money to find a model that you feel confident using and that complements your existing style of putting.

As with the rest of the clubs in your set, putters come with a variety of different shaft length options and lie angles, which means that once again you should take the time to try before you buy. A putter that inspires confidence when you hold it in your hands and look down at the ball is worth its weight in gold, so take your time choosing a make and model that you find inspirational.

USE THE SAME MAKE AND MODEL OF GOLF BALL FOR ULTIMATE CONSISTENCY

If you rummaged around inside the average amateur's golf bag, the chances are that you

YOUR CLUB-FITTING CHECKLIST

Regularly check and change your grips – if they are worn or shiny, replace them immediately. Slippery grips lead to tentative swings and a loss of control over the shot.

Check your loft and lie angles once a year. Ask a club-fitter to check your clubs at the beginning of each year so that your equipment remains consistent.

Find the correct shaft for your swing – if your shafts are too flexible for your swing speed you will struggle to control the ball and most likely hit a lot of hooked and pulled shots. If your shafts are too stiff for your swing speed, you will struggle to generate enough power through impact to square the clubface and will most likely slice or push the ball to the right.

would find a real mixed bag of old golf balls, brand new ones and scuffed balls – all of different brands and construction type.

While I would recommend that you take the time to experiment with different types of golf balls to find one that you feel comfortable using, it is perhaps even more important that you stick to just one particular type of ball. There can be a huge difference in the playing characteristics of a pure distance ball to that of a more receptive and feel-orientated ball. After playing with the same ball for an extended period of time, you will improve your feel and get to know how the ball will react off the clubface with any given shot.

Simple course-management skills

Most amateur golf is littered with unforced errors. Simple mistakes such as trying to pitch the ball over a bunker instead of playing safely to the side, under-clubbing, not making allowances for the effects of the wind and taking on shots that you know you have little chance of executing, all add up during the course of a round, and you would be amazed to find how many strokes you could save immediately if you eliminated those errors from your game.

Good course management is about playing to your strengths and being aware of your limitations. Put into simple terms, course management is the skill of plotting your way around the golf course in the most sensible manner, keeping the ball in play and away from trouble, at the same time as maximizing the use of your strengths.

KNOW YOUR YARDAGES WITH EVERY CLUB IN THE BAG

Knowing how far you hit the ball with each club in the bag is vital information that will determine your strategy on every shot. Without that knowledge at your disposal, your club selection on any shot is nothing more than guesswork.

Finally, do not let your ego get in the way of recording your accurate yardage. Most amateur golfers claim that they can hit their 7-iron 150 yards, but when you consider that Nick Price only hits his 155 yards, it is highly unlikely that the average club golfer is just five yards behind. In fact, most amateurs are closer to 130 yards with their 7-iron.

Take ten balls onto the practice field. After hitting all ten balls, walk up the range – ideally with a yardage wheel. Ignoring your two best and worst shots, measure the remaining six balls and take an average of the combined total. Like it or not, that is your yardage with that club. Repeat the process with every club in the bag. It will be one of your most productive practice sessions ever.

DISCOVER YOUR STOCK SHOT AND KNOW YOUR WEAKNESSES

You do not require a text-book technique to become a single-figure golfer. In many cases, a repetitive swing – one that you can rely on to create the same shape of shot every time – is good enough for you to keep the ball in play and avoid trouble.

In order to become a single-figure golfer, you will need to develop a stock shot that you can rely on in any imaginable pressure situation. It is also a very good idea to be aware of your swing flaws. Even the very best golfers have certain little idiosyncrasies that constantly return to haunt them.

Acquaint yourself with your own Achilles heel so that you will know what to look out for and how it will affect your game. Sometimes it is difficult to work out where your game is being let down, but the ability to diagnose the cause of your bad shots is invaluable.

MAKE A BOGEY YOUR WORST SCORE ON ANY HOLE

Damage limitation plays a key role in becoming a single-figure golfer. As I have mentioned already, you do not have to play flawless golf to reach a good standard. At this level of the game, you will still make bogeys. However, the skill is ensuring that you avoid the disaster scores, particularly where you drop two or more shots at a hole as a result of sloppy thinking and planning.

The key to keeping your scores low is adopting the principle that even though you might not make a par, your worst score at any given hole will be a bogey. Colin Montgomerie often says that bogeys add up slowly on the scorecard while doubles and triples add up very quickly indeed.

You should be aware that adopting this strategy does not mean that you should accept that you are going to drop a shot any time you find yourself in a bit of trouble on the course. What it means is that you should not compound errors by making several

more. In other words, you should always choose to play for safety rather than go for a risky shot.

USE YOUR FAVOURITE CLUB IN PRESSURE SITUATIONS

During every round of golf, there will be times when you have to play a pressure shot. In these kinds of situations, it is often advisable to boost your confidence by using your favourite club to play the shot so that you are more confident when you are standing over the ball. This is a particularly good ploy to help you overcome first-tee nerves. Rather than attempting to hit the shot with your driver, why not use your 4-iron, 5-iron or even your 7-iron to play the shot instead? It is far better to be 150 yards or so straight down the middle of the fairway than 180 yards in the trees.

NEVER RELY ON YOUR BEST SHOT TO CLEAR A HAZARD

Whenever there is a lake or other hazard guarding the green, you have two options: lay up short or play over it. Regardless of which decision you make, it is critical to know how far it is to reach the water and, also, how far it is to clear the hazard. That may sound like common sense, but you will be amazed at how many golfers make their decision without knowing either yardage. If you are going to lay up, make sure that you do not leave the ball right at the water's edge. If you go for the carry, do not rely on your best shot to make it. Always make it a comfortable shot, not one that is right at the limit of the club in your hand.

KEEP THE BALL LOW AROUND THE GREENS WHERE POSSIBLE

One of the most common and costliest amateur errors in all aspects of the game is attempting to play a fancy shot when a straightforward shot is easier and will get the job done just as well. Nowhere is this more important than when you are chipping from around the green. If there are no obstacles, such as rough, long grass, any kind of ditch or uneven ground between your ball and the hole, there is no point whatsoever trying to loft the ball into the air. The basic equation to remember is: 'less loft = less wrists = less margin for error.'

GET PIN HIGH WITH APPROACH SHOTS TO TAKE THE PRESSURE OFF YOUR PUTTING

One of the main reasons why it is so important to know how far you hit each club is so that you can reach pin high with your approach shots into the green. If you can get the ball level with the hole, a shot that is ten yards off line will only be 30 feet away from the hole, leaving you with a decent chance to hole the putt. If your approach shot is ten yards off line and also ten yards short, it is very likely that your ball will be off the green and you will be faced with an awkward chip or pitch to save your par.

TAKE THE PRESSURE OFF YOUR LONG-RANGE PUTTING

You do not have to go for the hole on every single medium- to long-range putt. Most golfers three-putt far too often and the main reason for this is under or over-hitting the first approach putt. You can remove a lot of the pressure in these situations by visualizing a circular zone 18 inches around the hole into which you should roll the ball. It does not really matter whether your putt finishes 18 inches short, long, left or right of the hole, because all of these shots are a tap-in.

QUICK TIP

WATCH A DVD OF A GOLF TOURNAMENT

To help you gain a better understanding of how you should play on the golf course, watch a golf tournament on television and carefully observe how the players plot their way around the course. See how they stick to their routines even under the severest pressure and how they negotiate their way out of trouble when they run into it.

HOW TO CLOSE OUT ON THE GREENS

Many things go through your mind after you have played a poor approach putt that leaves you an awkward distance of three or four feet from the hole. You may feel angry with yourself. But, whatever state you are in, it is unlikely to help you concentrate on the shot at hand. You can eliminate many missed short putts simply by restoring a positive mental state and concentrating on your normal pre-putt routine.

How to practise effectively

With only ten weeks to achieve your goal of becoming a single-figure player, you will need to set aside time for regular practice.

In the second section of this book, I will be demonstrating the practice exercises, drills and routines that will enable you to target your problem areas and enhance all aspects of your game. In most cases, you will have a set number of exercises to perform in order for you to quickly incorporate the new techniques into your game. However, in order to sustain your improvement once the plan finishes, or even to enhance and accelerate your progress during the ten weeks itself, you will need to know how to practise effectively.

To most golfers, practice means hitting balls, but that is simply exercising. In order to make your practice pay dividends, you must have a goal for each session.

DEVELOP A DAILY PRACTICE ROUTINE – AND STICK TO IT

As is the case with setting goals, the more detailed and structured you can make your practice schedule the better. During your ten week improvement plan you will be required to work on at least one aspect of your game every day. I recommend that you set aside a certain time each day for your practice. Write it in your diary and plan the rest of your schedule around it.

REMEMBER THAT QUALITY IS BETTER THAN QUANTITY

We all know how tempting it is to pick up the driver and start belting balls down the practice range, but aimlessly hitting balls into the distance does not do your game much good. Since most golfers probably have both a full-time job and other commitments that take up the majority of their life, time on the practice range is precious, and that means that you need to work at maximum efficiency.

The next time you visit the driving range opt for the medium-sized basket and aim to make the balls last for as long as it normally takes you to get through a larger one. Take your time over every shot and have a focus for every shot you hit – a feeling, a swing, or a particular shape or trajectory of shot.

DO NOT ALLOW BAD SHOTS TO DISTRACT YOU FROM YOUR PRACTICE GOAL

The purpose of practice is not necessarily to hit good shots. It is often the case that when you are tweaking some of your basics or introducing a new move or feeling into your swing, you may not strike the ball as well as you would like. That is not too important at this stage and you should not revert to your old swing simply to produce some acceptable shots. If the purpose of your practice session is to improve the wrist action in your backswing, for example, that is your priority and not perfect ball-striking.

SPEND MORE TIME PRACTISING YOUR SHORT GAME

The world's top professionals spend as much time chipping and putting around the practice greens as they do on the range working on their long game. They know that it is the quality of their short game that allows them to post seriously low scores.

You should devote at least as much time to refining your chipping and pitching techniques and your touch and feel as you do to practising your swing and your long game. A great short game can compensate for an errant long game, but the equation does not work the other way round.

USE PRACTICE TIME TO DEVELOP ROUTINES AS WELL AS TECHNIQUE

Practice is not just about hitting golf balls. Use your time on the range to create and groove the pre-shot routines that you will rely on to improve the consistency of your game. While it is unnecessary to go through your pre-shot routine on every single shot, it is a good idea to spend about 20 per cent of your practice time making your pre-shot preparation as slick and consistent as possible.

Many top golfers will hit ten balls while working on a specific swing thought, then hit three or four shots going through their whole routine, then finally revert to hitting balls and concentrating on a specific swing thought.

GETTING FIT FOR GOLF

Improved fitness levels among professional golfers are becoming an increasingly important aspect of the game. Think of how many times you have struggled to hold your game together over the final few holes of a round or how you have flagged towards the end of your week's golfing holiday. Although I'm not going to advocate regular sessions in the gym, I cannot stress highly enough how an improved level of fitness would benefit your game.

Carry energy snacks and water in your golf bag at all times

Many of the world's top golfers and tennis players can often be seen eating fruit – bananas in particular – since the carbohydrates and natural sugar found in these foods are released and absorbed more slowly into your system, thereby enabling you to sustain your energy levels for a longer period of time.

It is also advisable to carry a bottle of water in your golf bag. Dehydration is one of the main causes of deterioration in technique and it affects your body for a long while before you actually begin to see any physical signs. Drinking water throughout the round enables you to maintain your concentration levels and your ability to think clearly. Fizzy drinks may quench your thirst, but they do not provide you with sufficient replacement energy nor do they adequately prevent dehydration.

During this 10-week period, swap your chocolate bar and fizzy drink for a couple of bananas, an apple and a bottle of water and/or an energy drink.

During the following 10-week plan you will work on and develop all the key aspects of your game. Starting with a full review of the basic fundamentals, you will progress to learning the basic swing motion and then target the areas of the game that will enable you to make the most immediate and noticeable improvement to your scoring. For this reason, many of the putting and short-game techniques are covered very early in the programme, since it is on and around the greens where you can improve very quickly.

Each week of the plan focuses on a different department of the game. In addition to an explanation of the basic techniques, you will be asked to perform an accompanying selection of practice exercises and drills that can be found in Section 3. These exercises are specially chosen to accelerate your progress by grooving the correct swing feelings and movements. It is important that you perform at least the recommended number of repetitions of each exercise to fully incorporate the new moves into your game. There is nothing wrong with performing more repetitions if you have the time, but you should always bear in mind that it is the quality of your practice and not always the quantity that will determine how quickly you improve.

The performance-analysis table is the foundation of your 10-week game-improvement plan. It shows you how accomplished you should be in each area of the game, provides a record of your progress and helps you identify your weaknesses. Keeping detailed statistics will pinpoint problem areas and allow you to target your practice.

Record your statistics during each round and write down every shot and your score on each hole. Compare these with the recommended standard and identify the areas that cause you problems then turn to the practice exercises. As well as practising the daily exercises in the 10-week plan, you must continue to follow the relevant exercises from this table.

PERFORMANCE ANALYSIS

CATEGORY	TARGET	GO TO PAGE(S)	CATEGORY	TARGET	GO TO PAGE(S)
Drives over 200 yards	70%	74–83, 85, 87, 99–103	Approach putts short of the hole	1	126–134
Fairways hit	60%	74–83, 84–94, 99–102	Short putts missed (under 4 feet)	1	135–137
Greens in regulation total	11/18	74–83	Approach shots short of green	2	74–98
Greens in regulation – par-3s	75%	147, 90–98	Sand saves greenside bunkers	30%	120–125
Greens in regulation – par-4s	60%	150, 90–102	Chip shot up and downs	60%	114–120
Greens in regulation – par-5s	80%	153, 90–98	Total pitch shots 40–70 yards	6	108–114
Total putts per round	32	126–137	Up and downs 40–70 yards	40%	108–125, 135–137
Three-putts from long range	1	126–134	Course-management errors	0	138–155
Three-putts from short range	0	135–137			

COMPILE YOUR STATS

ROUND: DATE: GOLF COURSE:

USE FOR EACH HOLE

Fairway hit
☐ YES ☐ NO ☐ NOT APPLICABLE

Green in regulation
☐ YES ☐ NO

Approach shot/tee shot short of green
☐ YES ☐ NO

Chip shot up and down
☐ YES ☐ NO ☐ NOT APPLICABLE

Chip to within five feet and holed putt
☐ YES ☐ NO ☐ NOT APPLICABLE

Chip to within five feet and missed putt
☐ YES ☐ NO ☐ NOT APPLICABLE

Sand save in two shots
☐ YES ☐ NO ☐ NOT APPLICABLE

Sand save in three shots
☐ YES ☐ NO ☐ NOT APPLICABLE

NUMBER OF TOTAL PUTTS

Three-putt
☐ YES ☐ NO

Three-putt from long range
☐ YES ☐ NO ☐ NOT APPLICABLE

Three-putt from short range
☐ YES ☐ NO ☐ NOT APPLICABLE

Approach putt short of hole
☐ YES ☐ NO ☐ NOT APPLICABLE

Putt holed within ten feet
☐ YES ☐ NO ☐ NOT APPLICABLE

Putt holed 10-20 feet
☐ YES ☐ NO

Putt missed from short range
☐ YES ☐ NO

Pitch shot played
☐ YES ☐ NO

Pitch shot up and down in two
☐ YES ☐ NO ☐ NOT APPLICABLE

Pitch shot up and down in three
☐ YES ☐ NO ☐ NOT APPLICABLE

OVERALL PERFORMANCE

18-hole total ☐
Fairways hit ☐
Greens in regulation ☐
Total putts ☐
Approach shots short of the green ☐

Total three-putts ☐
Total up and downs ☐
Sand saves ☐
Pitch shot saves ☐
Short putts missed ☐

NOTES AND HIGHLIGHTS OF THE ROUND

OVERALL Driving good. Iron play average, but putting is improving. Found fewer bunkers, but more chip shots.

HIGHLIGHT OF THE ROUND Hitting tee shot at the tricky par-3 12th hole to two feet. Unfortunately, I missed the putt.

WEEK **1** > # All about address

The first week of your game-improvement programme is devoted entirely to the set-up. This is because all of the routines and practice exercises highlighted in the 10-week plan are based on the assumption that you possess a thorough understanding of the basic fundamentals of the game. Only once you have a solid and consistent address position can you begin to develop your game in all of the key areas. The vast majority of swing faults originate from flaws at address so it is vital that you understand the importance of developing a solid foundation = your swing.

YOUR FIRST WEEK

Your first week is key to this programme; the way you approach the first week will affect the way you approach the entire plan and will subsequently affect your rate of improvement over the next few months. Spend as much time as you possibly can working on all aspects of your set-up so that you can maximize the effectiveness of the exercises included in the schedule.

STRUCTURED PRACTICE

The first week of the plan will enable you to develop the fundamentals required to form the foundation of a solid and repetitive swing. Starting with forming the correct grip, you will go on to develop an athletic posture and good alignment and you will learn the correct width of stance and ball position for each club. The week's practice will culminate in a recommended pre-shot routine that will enable you to link all of the elements of your set-up into one continuous motion.

It is vital that you continue to practise, refine and rehearse your pre-shot routine throughout the duration of the 10-week plan. Your ultimate goal is to groove your preparation to such an extent that you are able subconsciously to settle into the correct address position each and every time you take a shot for maximum efficiency and effectiveness. A good address position also gives you the mental confidence that comes from good balance.

PERSONALIZED PRACTICE

In addition to the daily practice routines and exercises, you will also be able to target weaknesses in other areas of your game by using the performance-analysis table on page 28. Check your statistics in the key areas of the game and compare them with the guidelines on the table.

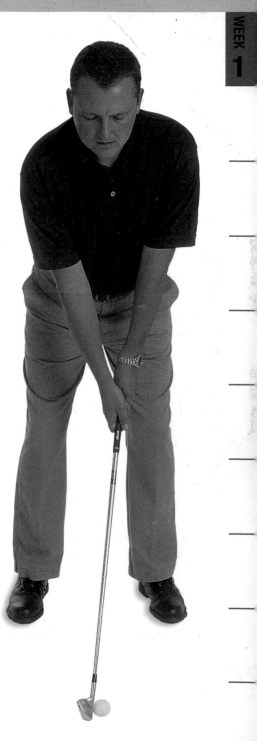

WEEK
1

THIS WEEK'S PRIORITIES

Monday   Building a neutral grip
Tuesday   Posture
Wednesday Stance and ball position
Thursday   Alignment
Friday   The address routine
Weekend   Putting it all together

GOAL FOR THE WEEK

Your goal for this week is to make sure that your set-up and pre-shot routine become both second nature and one continuous flowing motion rather than a series of linked positions. Although you should focus on the address routine in the first week, ideally you should make time every week to remind yourself of the correct sequence of movements. Most swing flaws can be traced back to an anomaly at address; therefore, the more errors you can eliminate at the set-up stage, the better your game will be in the long run.

BUILDING A NEUTRAL GRIP

The way in which you hold the club determines how good a player you can become. Unless you have had regular lessons from a PGA qualified instructor, it is likely that your grip will contain flaws. If this is the case, it is almost certain that you will make compensations for an incorrect grip in your swing, and this will lead to stroke inconsistency. A good grip does not in itself guarantee a good swing, but it does maximize your chances of squaring the clubface at impact to deliver a powerful strike to the ball. If your grip is unorthodox, holding the club correctly will initially feel awkward and uncomfortable and may result in poor play as your confidence and timing suffer until your body acclimatizes to the changes. However, it is vital that you adhere to the changes and practise forming your new grip as often as possible.

ASSIGNMENTS

❶ Take your clubs to a specialist club-fitter and check the loft and lie angles.

❷ Play a full round of golf and make a note of the key statistics and compare your current performance levels with the performance-analysis table.

PRACTICE EXERCISES

Grip 1 – 20 repetitions (p 74)

Grip 2 – 10 repetitions (p 75)

Grip 3 – 10 repetitions (p 76)

Grip 4 – As many repetitions as possible (p 77)

PERFECT YOUR POSTURE

A good posture is important for golf because the angles that you create in your lower spine and your legs will determine not only the shape and plane of your swing but also your ability to coil your shoulders correctly and generate power.

One of the key things to remember about your posture is that you should keep your spine as straight as possible, so that your upper body has a fixed point around which it can rotate back and through. You will struggle to coil powerfully if your spine is curved and your shoulders are slumped. The purpose of the golf posture is to create a position from which you can make an athletic swing at the ball.

ASSIGNMENT

❶ Check your set-up and posture in front of a mirror and compare it with that of a top player of a similar build, using a golf magazine or an instruction book for reference.

PRACTICE EXERCISES

Posture 1 – 20 repetitions (p 84)

Posture 2 – 10 repetitions with each club (p 85)

Posture 3 – Repeat regularly to check quality of posture (p 86)

Grip 1 – 20 repetitions (p 74)

Grip 3 – 10 repetitions (p 76)

Grip 4 – As many repetitions as possible (p 77)

STANCE AND BALL POSITION

Many amateurs make the mistake of keeping the same width of stance and ball position for every shot, regardless of whether they are hitting a driver or a pitching wedge. Understand that you need a wider stance to support the increased swing speed when hitting a driver or fairway wood and that you need to play the ball further forward in your stance to deliver a shallower attack into the ball. At the same time, your stance should be fairly narrow when hitting shorter irons and the ball should be played in the middle of the feet to encourage a steeper attack.

ASSIGNMENT

❶ Purchase a dozen golf balls – ask the pro or retailer to recommend a particular type/brand that is suitable for your game. Stick with the same construction type throughout the 10-week plan.

PRACTICE EXERCISES

Ball position 1 – 10 repetitions (p 87)
Ball position 2 – 10 repetitions (p 88)
Ball position 3 – 20 repetitions (p 89)
Posture 1 – 20 repetitions (p 84)
Posture 3 – Repeat regularly to check quality of posture (p 86)
Grip 1 – 20 repetitions (p 74)
Grip 3 – 10 repetitions (p 76)
Grip 4 – As many repetitions as possible (p 77)

UNDERSTANDING THE CONCEPT OF GOOD ALIGNMENT

Good alignment is one of the most important keys to success in golf, yet many amateur golfers ignore it completely and then wonder why their shots fail to find the target. It stands to reason that unless you take care in setting the clubface and your body to the target correctly, you will struggle to hit the ball where you want it to go. Understand that aiming the clubface is the first and most important part of your pre-shot routine. You can then use the clubface as a reference point around which you can position your feet and body correctly. Remember also that while the clubface aims at your intended target, the rest of your body aims square to that line, but not at it. This is known as parallel alignment.

ASSIGNMENTS

❶ Hit 50 balls at the driving range going through the full address routine before each and every shot.
❷ Watch a DVD of a golf tournament and see how the top professionals adhere to their pre-shot routine, even under the severest pressure.

PRACTICE EXERCISES

Alignment 1 – 20 repetitions (p 80)
Alignment 2 – 20 repetitions (p 82)
Alignment 3 – Use to double-check alignment when necessary (p 83)
Ball position 1 – 10 repetitions (p 87)
Ball position 2 – 10 repetitions (p 88)
Ball position 3 – 20 repetitions (p 89)

DEVELOP YOUR ADDRESS ROUTINE

It is important to develop an address routine so that you maximize your chances of standing to the ball correctly each and every time. Consistent preparation allows you to hit every shot from the same position, which is vital for ball-striking consistency and fault analysis. Enhance and develop your address routine using the points covered so that you can address the ball in the same way each time.

PRACTICE EXERCISES
Grip 1 – 10 repetitions (p 74)
Grip 3 – 10 repetitions (p 76)
Grip 4 – As many repetitions as possible (p 77)
Pre-shot routine 1 – 10 repetitions (p 78)
Pre-shot routine 2 – Repeat regularly (p 80)
Posture 1 – 10 repetitions (p 84)
Posture 2 – 10 repetitions with each club (p 85)
Posture 3 – Repeat regularly to check quality of posture (p 86)
Ball position 1 – 5 repetitions (p 87)
Ball position 2 – 5 repetitions (p 88)
Ball position 3 – 5 repetitions (p 89)
Alignment 1 – 10 repetitions (p 80)
Alignment 2 – 10 repetitions (p 82)
Alignment 3 – Use to double-check alignment when necessary (p 83)

DEVELOP AN ENTIRE PRE-SHOT ROUTINE

Now you know what a good address position looks and feels like, you can turn this position into part of an overall pre-shot routine to develop consistency. Make the address routine one free-flowing motion. From visualizing your shot to starting your swing, the movements involved should be seamless.

ASSIGNMENTS
❶ Play a round, keeping stats on key areas.
❷ Check your statistic against the performance-analysis table to identify any major weakness.
❸ Hit 40 balls at the driving range going through a full pre-shot routine before every shot.

PRACTICE EXERCISES
Pre-shot routine 1 – 15 repetitions (p 78)
Grip 1 – 10 repetitions (p 74)
Grip 3 – 10 repetitions (p 76)
Grip 4 – Repeat regularly (p 77)
Posture 1 – 10 repetitions (p 84)
Posture 2 – 10 repetitions with each club (p 85)
Posture 3 – Repeat regularly (p 86)
Ball position 1 – 5 repetitions (p 87)
Ball position 2 – 5 repetitions (p 88)
Ball position 3 – 5 repetitions (p 89)
Alignment 1 – 10 repetitions (page 80)
Alignment 2 – 10 repetitions (page 82
Alignment 3 – Use to double-check alignment when necessary (page 83)

Simplifying the swing

After Week 1 and once you have developed a sound understanding of the basic fundamentals, you can begin to develop your swing so that it is technically more proficient and, in turn, more consistent, reliable and powerful.

YOUR SECOND WEEK

Your second week builds on the foundations established in the first week of the plan. Depending on the severity of any ingrained address faults, you may still need to refine your basics and rehearse your address routines while you build and improve your swing.

STRUCTURED PRACTICE

The practice routines you will be asked to perform during this week will enable you to develop the key components of the golf swing – the upper body pivot, the arm swing, the wrist action and the resistance of the lower body and the right knee – and then blend them into one controlled and co-ordinated movement.

PERSONALIZED PRACTICE

In addition to the daily recommended routines, you should also perform the relevant practice exercises as prescribed by the performance-analysis table on page 28.

THIS WEEK'S PRIORITIES

Monday	The upper body pivot
Tuesday	The swinging of the arms
Wednesday	How and when to hinge your wrists
Thursday	The role of the lower body
Friday	Developing good rhythm
Weekend	Restoring the spontaneity

GOAL FOR THE WEEK

Your goal for this week is to develop a clearer understanding of the key elements that combine to form a solid and repetitive golf swing and to blend those elements together into one free-flowing, uninhibited motion.

COILING CORRECTLY

The coiling motion of the upper body is the core of any good golf swing. If the upper body rotates correctly around your spine angle then you have a very good chance of creating power and striking the ball cleanly. Your aim is to experience the feelings associated with the correct body pivot and, in particular, how the upper body coils around the spine angle introduced at address against the resistance of the lower body and, in particular, the right knee and thigh.

ASSIGNMENTS
❶ Perform some gentle stretching exercises to prepare your golfing muscles for the practice exercises you are about to perform.
❷ Hit 30 balls at the driving range, going through a full pre-shot routine before each shot.

PRACTICE EXERCISES
Swing drill 1 – 20 repetitions (p 90)
Swing drill 2 – 20 repetitions (p 91)
Grip 1 – 20 repetitions (p 74)
Grip 4 – As many repetitions as possible (p 77)
Posture 1 – 20 repetitions (p 84)

CREATE POWER WITH YOUR ARMS

Your arms create width, power and leverage in the swing, yet many amateur golfers fail to make full use of this key power source. As your upper body coils and turns back and through, your arms swing up and down. Restore the freedom of movement in your swing with a natural and uninhibited swinging motion with the arms. Feel as though your hands are directly above your right shoulder at the top of the swing.

ASSIGNMENTS
❶ Play a round of golf and keep statistics on key areas of the game.
❷ Purchase a cut-down or junior club so that you can practise your golf swing indoors at any time.

PRACTICE EXERCISES
Swing drill 3 – 30 repetitions (p 93)
Swing tempo 2 – 20 repetitions (p 97)
Swing drill 1 – 20 repetitions (p 90)
Swing drill 2 – 20 repetitions (p 91)
Practice swing drill – 20 repetitions (p 92)
Grip 1 – 20 repetitions (p 74)
Grip 4 – As many repetitions as possible (p 77)
Posture 1 – 20 repetitions (p 84)

ACTIVATING YOUR WRISTS

Together with the swinging motion of your arms, the wrists are another source of power that many golfers fail to utilize correctly. Good wrist action plays an important role in enabling the club to find the correct plane in the backswing so that it can approach the ball on the correct angle and path. Active wrist action brings improved control in the swing. Learn what the correct wrist action feels like and blend that wrist action into the overall motion so that it becomes an instinctive and integral part of your swing.

ASSIGNMENT

❶ Make plenty of practice swings without a ball, while allowing your wrists to hinge freely on the backswing and then again on the follow-through so that you get used to a lively hand action in the swing.

PRACTICE EXERCISES

Practice swing drill – 20 repetitions (p 92)
Swing drill 3 – 20 repetitions (p 93)
Swing drill 4 – 20 repetitions (p 94)
Angle drill – 20 repetitions (p 95)
Grip 3 – 20 repetitions (p 76)
Grip 4 – As many repetitions as possible (p 77)
Posture 1 – 20 repetitions (p 84)

STABILIZING THE SWING

Just as a generator needs a fixed base in order to create power, so the golf swing requires similar stability. Your lower body – legs, hips and feet – is the support of your swing as well as a key source of power. If your lower body gives way during the backswing, you will be unable to coil your shoulders correctly and create maximum power. The right knee remains flexed and resists the coiling motion of the torso during the backswing. While the upper body turns, the arms swing and the wrists hinge during the backswing, the right knee remains flexed and almost stationary.

ASSIGNMENT

❶ Hit 40 balls at the range going through a full pre-shot routine on half of the shots. With the other 20 balls, perform three repetitions of any recommended swing drill without a ball before hitting a shot for real.

PRACTICE EXERCISES

Swing drill 1 – 20 repetitions (p 90)
Swing drill 2 – 20 repetitions (p 91)
Swing drill 3 – 30 repetitions (p 93)
Swing tempo 2 – 20 repetitions (p 97)
Grip 3 – 20 repetitions (p 76)
Grip 4 – As many repetitions as possible (p 77)
Posture 1 – 20 repetitions (p 84)

WEEK 2

BLENDING THE SWING MOTION – DEVELOPING RHYTHM

Once you have developed all of the key areas of the golf swing, the next step is to blend those individual elements together into one free-flowing motion. No matter how technically accomplished you are, unless your swing has a good rhythm and tempo, it will simply be a series of disjointed motions. Combine the upper body pivot, the swinging motion of the arms, the correct wrist action and lower body resistance into one free-flowing and controlled motion.

ASSIGNMENTS

❶ Hit 50 balls at the driving range, going through the full pre-shot routine on at least half the shots. On the remaining 25 balls, perform one pivot, wrist action, arm swing and lower body resistance exercise before hitting each shot.

❷ Match your swing tempo to your general personality. For example, the laid-back Ernie Els swings slowly and languidly while the more sprightly Sergio Garcia has a quick-fire swing.

PRACTICE EXERCISES

Swing drill 1 – 20 repetitions (p 90)
Swing drill 2 – 20 repetitions (p 91)
Swing drill 3 – 30 repetitions (p 93)
Swing tempo 1 – 10 repetitions (p 96)
Swing tempo 2 – 10 repetitions (p 97)
Swing tempo 3 – 10 repetitions (p 98)

RESTORING THE FLAIR AND SPONTANEITY

When working on your swing it is very easy to fall into the trap of becoming too position-orientated, often to the extent that you may find it difficult to swing rhythmically as you have too many thoughts in your head. One of the keys to improving your swing is to focus on technique at the practice range and then restrict yourself to just one key swing thought when you go out to play. Extend your pre-shot routine so that it now incorporates the visualization of the shot, the address routine and the golf swing itself. The routine is over once the ball has left the clubface.

ASSIGNMENTS

❶ Play a round of golf and keep statistics on key areas of the game. Compare your performance against the performance-analysis table.

❷ Hit 50 balls at the range going through a pre-shot routine with at least half the balls. With the remaining 25 balls, you should make several practice swings before hitting each shot and focus on one thought when you hit the ball.

PRACTICE EXERCISES

Swing drill 1 – 20 repetitions (p 90)
Swing drill 2 – 20 repetitions (p 91)
Swing drill 3 – 30 repetitions (p 93)
Swing tempo 1 – 10 repetitions (p 96)
Swing tempo 2 – 10 repetitions (p 97)
Swing tempo 3 – 10 repetitions (p 98)

WEEK 3 ▶ Perfecting your putting

Putting is a crucial part of becoming a single-figure golfer, since the ability to hole crucial putts will keep your score ticking over, while avoiding three-putts will take a lot of the pressure off your long game. For this reason, and the fact that around half the shots you play during a round of golf are on the green, putting appears very early in the plan.

GOAL FOR THE WEEK
Your goal for this week is to develop a repetitive putting stroke that will enable you to strike the ball solidly each time and a pre-putt routine that will enable you to set up to the ball and read the greens in a consistent manner.

YOUR THIRD WEEK
Your third week focuses on the skills you need to develop to become a consistently good putter. Developing confidence on the greens is crucial to your success as a golfer.

STRUCTURED PRACTICE
Good putting is a chain reaction that starts as soon as you read the putt. You will learn a green-reading routine, develop a consistent putting stroke and improve your feel for distance from long range and your ability to hole out successfully from within six feet of the hole.

PERSONALIZED PRACTICE
In addition to the recommended daily exercises you should also perform the relevant exercises as prescribed by the performance-analysis table. It is vital that you devote as much time as possible to practising your putting. Simply by avoiding three-putting you will notice an immediate and significant improvement to your scoring.

THIS WEEK'S PRIORITIES
Monday	Refining your putting set-up
Tuesday	Developing the putting stroke
Wednesday	Learning to read greens
Thursday	Controlling the distance of your putts
Friday	Holing out from short range
Weekend	Putting it all together

WEEK 3

WEEK
3

THE PUTTING SET-UP

Although there are no set rules when it comes to putting, unless you play almost every day it pays to be as orthodox as possible. Good posture allows your arms to hang naturally from your shoulders so that you can control the motion of the stroke, while positioning your eyes as close as possible to directly over the ball will give you a better view of the line of the putt. Your target for the day is to adopt an athletic, solid and comfortable posture that will enable your head and lower body to remain steady as you make your stroke.

ASSIGNMENTS

❶ Check to see if the lie of your putter is correct. Ideally, there should be just enough room to slide a small coin between the ground and the toe of your putter at address.

❷ Hit 40 balls on the putting green, going through a full pre-shot routine on every shot you make.

PRACTICE EXERCISES

Putting address routine – 15 repetitions (p 126)

Putting posture – 15 repetitions (p 128)

Putting technique 2 – 15 repetitions (p 131)

THE PUTTING STROKE

The putting stroke is a very straightforward action that is often over-complicated by amateurs. The secret is to keep your head and lower body steady while the putter face remains low to the ground throughout the whole stroke. Eliminate all unnecessary and wasted movements from the putting stroke and develop a smooth and repetitive motion that enables you to strike the ball solidly and with authority every time.

ASSIGNMENTS

❶ Make sure your putter matches your stroke. If your stroke is long, loose and slow like that of Phil Mickelson, a bladed putter will probably suit you best, while a centre-shafted putter is more effective with a more compact and brisker stroke.

❷ Play a full round of golf and make a note of the key statistics and compare your current performance levels with the performance-analysis table.

PRACTICE EXERCISES

Putting address routine – 15 repetitions (p 126)

Putting stroke routine – 30 repetitions (p 127)

Putting technique 1 – 15 repetitions (p 129)

Putting technique 2 – 15 repetitions (p 131)

READING GREENS

Reading greens is a combination of judging the slope and pace of a putt. It is a skill that you develop over a period of time, but you can accelerate the learning process by being consistent in your preparation and application each time you find yourself on the green. Develop a consistent pre-putt routine that you should adhere to on each and every putt, regardless of its length or importance.

ASSIGNMENTS

❶ Test you green-reading skills by finding a sloping putt and placing a tee peg at the apex where you believe the ball will begin to break towards the hole. Hit several putts towards the peg, monitor your results and adjust your judgement as necessary.

❷ Learn how different putts will behave differently by hitting some uphill and downhill putts and watching the difference. Uphill putts break less than downhill putts.

PRACTICE EXERCISES

Reading greens – 15 repetitions (p 130)
Putting address routine – 15 repetitions (p 126)
Putting stroke routine – 20 repetitions (p 127)
Putting technique 1 – 15 repetitions (p 129)
Putting technique 2 – 10 repetitions (p 131)

LEARNING DISTANCE CONTROL

Once you have learned the basics of the stroke and reading greens, your next step is to adjust the length of your stroke to match putts of different distances. Leaving long-range putts short of the hole puts a lot of pressure on your putting. If you can develop a good feel for distance, you will notice an immediate improvement in your scoring. The most effective way to vary the distance you hit the ball is to either lengthen or shorten your putting stroke, not to attempt to hit the ball harder or more softly.

ASSIGNMENTS

❶ Hit 40 balls on the putting green going through a full pre-shot routine before every shot.

❷ To develop a more authoritative putting stroke, practise hitting putts uphill and then recreate the same length of stroke on a flat putt of the same length and monitor the result.

PRACTICE EXERCISES

Reading greens – 15 repetitions (p 130)
Putting address routine – 15 repetitions (p 126)
Putting stroke routine – 10 repetitions (p 127)
Putting technique 1 – 15 repetitions (p 129)
Putting technique 2 – 5 repetitions (p 131)
Putting feel 1 – 15 repetitions (p 132)
Putting feel 2 – 15 repetitions (p 133)
Putting feel 3 – 15 repetitions (p 134)

WEEK **3**

HOLING THE PRESSURE PUTTS

There are many reasons, including poor approach putts and indifferent chipping, why you may face several tricky three- or four-footers during a round. Hole them all and you keep your score ticking over nicely, miss them all and you feel that you've thrown shots away. Commit fully to every short putt and adopt a positive and authoritative attitude. Develop a square-to-square stroke where the putter moves straight back and through.

ASSIGNMENTS

❶ Test the quality of your alignment and stroke on short putts by drawing a line from the ball to the centre of the hole with a piece of chalk and aim to roll the ball along that line. Adjust your aim and alignment if you find this difficult to do.

❷ Make a pact with yourself that you will never quit on a short putt again. It is better to miss giving the putt a positive roll than to make a nervous and tentative stroke and never give the putt a chance to drop.

PRACTICE EXERCISES

Putting address routine – 15 repetitions (p 126)

Putting stroke routine – 10 repetitions (p 127)

Putting technique 2 – 5 repetitions (p 131)

Short putts 1 – 20 repetitions (p 135)

Short putts 2 – 20 repetitions (p 136)

Short putts 3 – 10 repetitions (p 137)

PUTTING IT ALL TOGETHER

Once you have learned the individual elements of putting, it is time to blend them together. Consistent putting is a chain reaction from the initial read of the putt to holing out. Make your pre-putt routine natural and instinctive. Hit every putt from the same position for consistency and become comfortable with putts of all lengths.

ASSIGNMENTS

❶ Time your green-reading routine and devote the same amount of time to each putt.

❷ On long putts, it is a good idea to make practice strokes while looking at the hole in order to feel the length of stroke.

❸ Play a round of golf and note the key statistics and compare your current performance levels with the analysis table.

PRACTICE EXERCISES

Putting address routine – 15 repetitions (p 126)

Putting stroke routine – 30 repetitions (p 127)

Putting technique 1 – 15 repetitions (p 129)

Reading greens – 15 repetitions (p 130)

Putting technique 2 – 15 repetitions (p 131)

Putting feel 1 – 15 repetitions (p 132)

Putting feel 2 – 15 repetitions (p 133)

Putting feel 3 – 15 repetitions (p 134)

Short putts 1 – 20 repetitions (p 135)

Short putts 2 – 20 repetitions (p 136)

Short putts 3 – 10 repetitions (p 137)

WEEK 4 ▸ # Chipping

All of the world's top golfers are masters at getting up and down in two shots from around the green and there is no reason why you cannot achieve a similar success rate. The chipping technique itself is relatively easy to master and from that point on the quality of your short game will depend primarily on your ability to visualize, judge and feel the shot.

YOUR FOURTH WEEK

During the fourth week you will learn a consistent and reliable chipping technique that will enable you to strike the ball cleanly each time and in turn allow you to develop an enhanced sense of touch and feel around the greens.

STRUCTURED PRACTICE

This week the practice schedule demonstrates how you should address the ball for a chip shot and explains how you should choke down on the club correctly for extra control without losing your posture. You will then learn a consistent chipping technique and perform exercises and drills to improve your feel for distance and your ability to visualize the shot in your mind before you play it.

PERSONALIZED PRACTICE

In addition to the recommended daily routines, you should supplement your daily practice with the relevant routines prescribed by the performance-analysis table on page 28.

THIS WEEK'S PRIORITIES

Monday	Chipping set-up
Tuesday	Chipping technique
Wednesday	Chipping distance control
Thursday	Improving your imagination
Friday	Holing the pressure putts
Weekend	Consolidating the week's activities

GOAL FOR THE WEEK

Your goal for this week is to develop a solid chipping technique so that you can play the shots proficiently enough to get up and down in two shots from anywhere around the green on a regular basis and, even more importantly, ensure that you never take more than three shots to get the ball into the hole.

WEEK 4

SETTING UP FOR THE CHIP SHOT

The key to successful chipping is in the set-up. Placing your weight on the front foot and playing the ball back of centre in the stance makes it easier to strike the ball cleanly each time and therefore reduces the risk of mishitting or fluffing shots around the green. Familiarize yourself with the correct chipping address position so that it feels both comfortable and natural.

ASSIGNMENT

❶ Watch a golf event on television and see how the top players always try to keep the ball low to the ground where possible around the green.

PRACTICE EXERCISES

Chipping 1 – 20 repetitions (p 114)
Chipping 2 – 10 repetitions (p 116)

THE BASIC CHIP SHOT

This is the shot to play around the green when there are no hazards blocking the route from your ball to the hole. The general idea is to loft the ball onto the green where it can roll the rest of the way to the hole along the ground, just like a putt. Develop a short and compact chipping technique where you control the shot with your arms and shoulders and keep your wrist action to a minimum.

ASSIGNMENTS

❶ To see why keeping the ball low to the ground is the safest option, stand just off the edge of the green and roll three balls to the hole. Now take three more balls and this time try to land them next to the hole by throwing them into the air. The first three balls will invariably finish much closer to the hole.

❷ Play a full round of golf and make a note of the key statistics and compare your current performance levels with the performance-analysis table.

PRACTICE EXERCISES

Chipping 1 – 20 repetitions (p 114)
Chipping 2 – 10 repetitions (p 116)
Chipping 3 – 10 repetitions (p 117)

CLUB SELECTION

Although many top players have a favourite club that they will use to play the majority of their chip shots, unless you play every day it is advisable to match the club to the shot in question. You can chip with anything from a 4-iron to a lob wedge. Familiarize yourself with the different carry/roll ratios that you can expect with any given club. For example a 4-iron will not carry very far but it will roll a long way once it hits the green, while with the same length swing a sand wedge will carry the ball a similar distance but it will stop much quicker on landing.

ASSIGNMENT
❶ Hit 40 balls on the putting green going through a full pre-shot routine with every shot.

PRACTICE EXERCISES
Chipping 1 – 20 repetitions (p 114)
Chipping 2 – 10 repetitions (p 116)
Chipping 3 – 10 repetitions (p 117)
Chipping feel 1 – 10 repetitions (p 118)
Chipping feel 2 – 20 repetitions (p 119)

DEVELOPING YOUR IMAGINATION

After you have developed a good technique and a sense for distance, a good imagination is the third ingredient for a sharp short game. Due to the almost infinite number of situations you can find yourself in around the green, it is inevitable that you will often need to improvise your technique to match the situation. Gain confidence in improvising your technique by changing your stance, your ball position, the angle of the clubface and even the swing itself to hit a variety of different shots.

ASSIGNMENTS
❶ Set aside ten minutes at the end of your practice session to have some fun attempting adventurous recovery shots. This will teach you what is and what is not possible around the greens.
❷ Arrange to practise your short game with a friend and add some competition into the session in order to recreate the pressure of a real on-course situation.

PRACTICE EXERCISES
Chipping 1 – 20 repetitions (p 114)
Chipping 2 – 10 repetitions (p 116)
Chipping 3 – 10 repetitions (p 117)
Chipping feel 1 – 10 repetitions (p 118)
Chipping feel 2 – 20 repetitions (p 119)
Chipping feel 3 – 20 repetitions (p 120)

WEEK **4**

HOLING OUT AND FINISHING THE JOB

Although your goal will be to knock every chip stone-dead to the hole, unfortunately, you will often leave the ball within that tricky four- to six-foot range. Holing out is as important as the chipping technique itself. Apply as much concentration to the putting element of the shot as you do to the chipping and learn how to plan ahead so that you leave yourself the easiest possible putt for your next shot.

ASSIGNMENT

❶ Hit 40 balls onto the putting green, going through a full pre-shot routine with every shot.

PRACTICE EXERCISES

Chipping 1 – 20 repetitions (p 114)
Chipping 2 – 10 repetitions (p 116)
Chipping 3 – 10 repetitions (p 117)
Short putts 1 – 10 repetitions (p 135)
Short putts 2 – 10 repetitions (p 136)

FINE-TUNING YOUR SHORT-GAME SKILLS

Devote your whole weekend to refining your chipping around the greens and your short-range putting. This is an area of the game where you can never get enough practice. Refine your chipping technique and develop your touch and feel as well as your imagination and repertoire of shots.

ASSIGNMENTS

❶ Hit 40 balls onto the putting green making sure to go through a full pre-shot routine with every shot.

❷ Play a full round of golf and make a note of the key statistics and compare your current performance levels with the performance-analysis table.

PRACTICE EXERCISES

Chipping 1 – 50 repetitions (p 114)
Chipping 2 – 30 repetitions (p 116)
Chipping 3 – 20 repetitions (p 117)
Chipping feel 1 – 20 repetitions (p 118)
Chipping feel 2 – 20 repetitions (p 119)
Chipping feel 3 – 20 repetitions (p 120)
Short putts 1 – 20 repetitions (p 135)
Short putts 2 – 20 repetitions (p 136)

WEEK 5 ▶ # The long game

Although a competent short game can often compensate for errant driving and approach play, improving your long game is without doubt the quickest way to improve your handicap. If you can carry the ball a reasonable distance off the tee with a good level of accuracy, the rest of the hole becomes easier because your next shot is played with a shorter and more controllable club. That inevitably means that you have a better chance of hitting the ball onto the green and closer to the hole. Improving the quality of your long game will have a knock-on effect for the rest of your game, which will inevitably lead to lower scores.

YOUR FIFTH WEEK

During this week you will learn how to maximize both your distance and accuracy off the tee and how to improve all aspects of your long game. You will also learn how to shape your shots and control their trajectory. You will find this skill particularly useful when playing in windy conditions or when faced with obstacles such as trees or bushes blocking your route to the green.

STRUCTURED PRACTICE

Starting with driving, the practice routines for this week show you how to amend your set-up in order to curve the ball in the air or to alter the flight of the ball.

PERSONALIZED PRACTICE

In addition to the daily practice routines, you should also perform the relevant exercises prescribed in the performance-analysis table. It is also a good idea to vary the shape and trajectory of your shots in order to give your brain a more detailed task to focus on during the swing.

THIS WEEK'S PRIORITIES

Monday	Driving and fairway woods
Tuesday	Long and short irons
Wednesday	Fade shots
Thursday	Draw shots
Friday	High shots and low shots
Weekend	Refining your shot-making skills

WEEK 5

GOAL FOR THE WEEK

To improve your driving technique so that you can regularly hit the fairway and carry the ball around 200 yards off the tee, and to improve your long game so that you can hit your approach shots onto the green around 50 per cent of the time.

WEEK 5

DRIVING – REFINE YOUR SET-UP

Most golfers' problems originate from inaccurate and badly struck tee shots, which are often the result of poor basics. The driver will magnify any glitch in your address position. Combat this by taking a wide stance for stability and set a little extra weight on your right side so you can make a full shoulder turn. Play the ball forward in your stance, roughly opposite your left instep so that you catch the ball slightly on the upswing at impact. Adopting the correct driving and fairway wood set-up improves your confidence level, so that you look forward to driving the ball off the tee and hitting fairway woods onto the green from all kinds of different lies.

ASSIGNMENTS
1 Play a round, and keep statistics on the key areas.
2 Check the performance-analysis table to identify any major weaknesses.
3 Practise teeing the ball at the correct height so that half of the ball is visible above the top of the driver.

PRACTICE EXERCISES
Alignment 1 – 10 repetitions (p 80)
Alignment 2 – 10 repetitions (p 82)
Posture 1 – 10 repetitions (p 84)
Posture 2 – 10 repetitions (p 85)
Ball position 1 – 10 repetitions (p 87)
Driver set-up – 10 repetitions (p 99)
Driver swing – 20 repetitions (p 100)
Driver backswing – 10 repetitions (p 102)

LONG AND SHORT IRONS

Although your swing should remain the same regardless of the particular club you are using, it is inevitable that the longer irons will be more difficult to control than the shorter irons. A crisply struck iron shot is less likely to be blown off line by the wind and will stop quickly once it hits the green. Concentrate on making the same swing with every iron club in the bag and develop the same level of confidence with your long irons as you have with your mid-irons and wedges.

ASSIGNMENTS
1 Hit 50 balls at the driving range, going through your new address routine prior to hitting each shot.
2 Work on your grip at home, continually gripping and re-gripping the club in the prescribed way until the process begins to feel both natural and comfortable.
3 Take a brisk 15-minute walk to improve your general fitness levels.
4 Perform recommended practice exercises/routines from the performance-analysis table.

PRACTICE EXERCISES
Alignment 1 – 10 repetitions (p 80)
Alignment 2 – 10 repetitions (p 82)
Posture 1 – 10 repetitions (p 84)
Posture 2 – 10 repetitions (p 85)
Ball position 2 – 10 repetitions (p 88)
Swing drill 1 – 10 repetitions (p 90)
Swing drill 2 – 10 repetitions (p 91)
Swing drill 3 – 10 repetitions (p 93)

HITTING A FADE SHOT

Many top players like a fade shot – where the ball moves from left to right in the air – as their stock shot, as it offers a high level of control and accuracy. The ball lands softly and is less likely to release and roll once it hits the green. Learn the changes that you need to make to your set-up in order to produce the left-to-right ball flight in the air and practise the shot so that you are confident in your ability to curve the ball at will.

ASSIGNMENTS

❶ Check your set-up and posture in front of a mirror and compare it with that of a top player with a similar build, using a golf magazine or book for reference.

❷ Perform recommended practice exercises/routines from the performance-analysis table.

PRACTICE EXERCISES

Shaping shots 1 – 30 repetitions (p 102)
Shaping shots 3 – 30 repetitions (p 105)
Swing drill 1 – 10 repetitions (p 90)
Swing drill 2 – 10 repetitions (p 91)
Swing drill 3 – 10 repetitions (p 93)

HITTING A DRAW

The draw may produce more distance than a fade, but the downside is that it is not so easy to control the topspin imparted on the ball. Most top players will use this shot off the tee either to maximize their distance or to take advantage of a dogleg, although it is a useful shot to have if you want to hit an approach shot to a pin tucked away in the back left corner of a green. Learn the changes you need to make to your set-up in order to produce the right-to-left ball flight and practise the shot until you can consistently curve the ball at will.

ASSIGNMENTS

❶ Hit 50 shots at the driving range, going through a full address routine before each shot, and focus on producing a particular shape of shot with each ball.

❷ Work on the grip at home, continually gripping and re-gripping the club until it begins to feel natural and comfortable.

❸ Continue to refine your basics and address position at home in front of a mirror.

❹ Perform recommended practice exercises/routines from the performance-analysis table.

PRACTICE EXERCISES

Shaping shots 2 – 30 repetitions (p 104)
Shaping shots 3 – 30 repetitions (p 105)
Swing drill 1 – 10 repetitions (p 90)
Swing drill 2 – 10 repetitions (p 91)
Swing drill 3 – 10 repetitions (p 93)

WEEK 5

HITTING HIGH AND LOW SHOTS

The ability to vary the trajectory of your shots will help you clear obstacles – such as trees or bushes – that block your route to the green and will also help either to take advantage of a downwind or reduce the effects of a headwind. Learn the changes that you need to make to your address position and your swing technique in order to produce a higher or lower ball flight.

REFINING YOUR SHOT-MAKING SKILLS

Many club golfers are too one-dimensional in their approach to the game. Better players have a variety of shot-making options at their disposal which enable them to cope with the different situations that they are likely to come up against on the course. Develop your shot-making skills so that you are comfortable hitting high and low shots as well as fades and draws.

WEEK **5**

ASSIGNMENTS

❶ Hit 50 balls at the driving range, going through a full address routine before each and every shot. Focus on hitting a combination of high and low shots as well as fades and draws.

❷ Watch a DVD of a golf tournament and see how the top professionals adhere to their pre-shot routines even under the severest pressure.

❸ Perform recommended practice exercises/routines from the performance-analysis table.

ASSIGNMENTS

❶ Play a round and keep statistics on the key areas.

❷ Check your statistics against the performance-analysis table to identify any major weaknesses.

❸ Experiment with different stances, ball positions and clubface angles at address and see how they affect the flight of the ball.

❹ Practise visualizing the shot in your mind and then manufacture a swing that will produce the desired flight.

PRACTICE EXERCISES

Trajectory 1 – 30 repetitions (p 106)
Trajectory 2 – 30 repetitions (p 107)
Trajectory 3 – 30 repetitions (p 108)
Swing drill 1 – 10 repetitions (p 90)
Swing drill 2 – 10 repetitions (p 91)
Swing drill 3 – 10 repetitions (p 93)

PRACTICE EXERCISES

Shaping shots 1 – 30 repetitions (p 102)
Shaping shots 2 – 30 repetitions (p 104)
Shaping shots 3 – 30 repetitions (p 105)
Trajectory 1 – 30 repetitions (p 106)
Trajectory 2 – 30 repetitions (p 107)
Trajectory 3 – 30 repetitions (p 108)
Swing drill 1 – 10 repetitions (p 90)
Swing drill 2 – 10 repetitions (p 91)
Swing drill 3 – 10 repetitions (p 93)

WEEK 6 ▶ **Pitching and bunker play**

Although pitching and bunker play are not the most crucial areas to target if you want to become a single-figure golfer, the ability to pitch the ball safely onto the green and to splash the ball confidently out of the sand first time will help you avoid dropping shots needlessly. Many strokes are wasted from within 70 yards of the flag purely because the golfer cannot land the ball on the green from this distance and instead leaves the ball short and then has to rely on another chip to get the ball close to the hole. The same situation applies to bunker play.

YOUR SIXTH WEEK
Your sixth week focuses on pitching into the green from within 60 to 70 yards – a key

scoring zone for many club golfers – and the skills required to recover safely from the sand at the first attempt.

STRUCTURED PRACTICE
The practice routines that you will be performing this week will enable you to develop a consistent pitching technique and a method for judging distance. You will also learn the basics of bunker play.

THIS WEEK'S PRIORITIES

Monday	Pitching – the basic technique
Tuesday	Pitching – judging distance
Wednesday	Bunker play– the set-up
Thursday	Bunker play – the swing
Friday	Holing out
Weekend	A review of the week's work

WEEK 6

GOAL FOR THE WEEK

Your goal for this week is first to develop a consistent pitching technique that will enable you to carry the ball through the air and onto the green from within 70 yards. The second part of your goal is to develop a bunker-play technique that will enable you to splash the ball out of the sand and onto the green at the first attempt and leave a putt for your next shot. Your goal is never to take more than three shots to get up and down with a pitch or bunker shot.

THE PITCH SHOT

The pitch shot is basically an abbreviated version of your full swing. Other than making some minor amendments to your set-up in order to reduce the distance you hit the ball, the swing is exactly the same as for a full shot. Good rhythm is the key to striking the ball consistently. Your aim is to master the changes you need to make to your address position and to develop a smooth pitching action that enables you to strike the ball crisply and cleanly each time.

ASSIGNMENTS

❶ Play a round of golf, keeping statistics on key areas of the game.

❷ Check the performance-analysis table to identify any major weaknesses.

PRACTICE EXERCISES

Pitching 1 – 20 repetitions (p 108)

Grip 1 – 10 repetitions (p 74)

Grip 2 – 10 repetitions (p 75)

Posture 1 – 20 repetitions (p 84)

Posture 2 – 20 repetitions (p 85)

Swing tempo 1 – 10 repetitions (p 96)

Swing tempo 2 – 10 repetitions (p 97)

PITCHING – JUDGING DISTANCE

Once you have developed the basic pitching technique, you need to learn to control the distance you hit the shot. Good pitching technique without distance control is worthless. You must be able to pitch the ball confidently onto the green every time. Your focus today is to develop a method of judging distance that will enable you to match the length and speed of your swing to the shot that you face.

ASSIGNMENTS

❶ Hit 50 balls at the driving range, going through your new address routine prior to hitting each shot.

❷ Continue to refine your basics. Focus on your posture as it is very easy to lose your spine angle and get slumped over the ball when pitching.

❸ Watch a DVD of a golf tournament and note how infrequently top players leave the ball short of the green with a pitch shot.

❹ Make a note of how far you carry the ball with a different length backswing and with different clubs when pitching.

PRACTICE EXERCISES

Pitching 1 – 20 repetitions (p 108)

Pitching 2 – 20 repetitions (p 110)

Pitching 3 – 20 repetitions (p 111)

Pitching 4 – 10 repetitions (p 112)

Grip 1 – 10 repetitions (p 74)

Grip 2 – 10 repetitions (p 75)

Posture 1 – 20 repetitions (p 84)

Posture 2 – 20 repetitions (p 85)

BUNKER PLAY – THE SET-UP

Even the very best players in the world will only get up and down in two shots from the sand about six or seven times out of ten, so there is no need for you to master this particular area of the game. However, you should reach a standard where you can get the ball out of the bunker and onto the green at the first attempt so that you leave a putt for your next shot. Learn what amendments you need to make to your address position and why. Rehearse the set-up routine so that it becomes second nature when you walk into a bunker.

ASSIGNMENTS

❶ Check that your sand wedge has a wide sole and that it feels slightly heavier than the rest of your irons. If it doesn't, consider exchanging it for a different make. The Ping sand wedge is widely recognized as one of the best for amateur golfers.

❷ Step into a bunker and fill a beaker or a pint glass with sand. This is the amount of sand you need to remove from the bunker when you play your shot. Feel how heavy it is.

PRACTICE EXERCISES

Bunker play address routine 1 –
20 repetitions (p 120)
Bunker play address routine 2 –
20 repetitions (p 122)

BUNKER PLAY – THE SWING

Once you have set up to the ball correctly in the bunker, the key is to swing along the line of your body, not the ball/target line. This will encourage the clubface to remain open through impact and will ensure that it slides underneath the ball rather than digging deeply into the sand. Learn the correct swing path and understand why you need to make almost a full swing to remove the ball from the sand.

ASSIGNMENTS

❶ Hit 30 shots at the driving range, going through a full address routine before each shot.

❷ Do not hit every practice bunker shot from a perfect lie. Hit some from bad lies in the bunker to recreate a realistic on-course situation.

❸ Watch a DVD of a golf tournament and study the bunker-play techniques of the top players. See how they take almost a full swing every time from the sand.

PRACTICE EXERCISES

Bunker play address routine 1 –
20 repetitions (p 120)
Bunker play address routine 2 –
20 repetitions (p 122)
Bunker play 1 – 20 repetitions (p 124)
Bunker play 2 – 20 repetitions (p 125)

**WEEK
6**

HOLING OUT WITH CONVICTION

Just as holing the return putt is a crucial part of your overall success at chipping, so your ability to hole putts from within five or six feet can make a huge difference to your score at the end of a round. Unless you are a very good bunker player, you will constantly leave yourself putts of around ten feet to save par. Develop a consistent and reliable putting stroke for dealing with short- to medium-length putts.

ASSIGNMENTS

❶ Hit 30 balls at the driving range, going through your address routine before each and every shot.

❷ Watch a DVD of a golf tournament and see how the top professionals approach short putts with confidence and how they strike the ball positively rather than dribbling the ball towards the hole.

PRACTICE EXERCISES

Bunker play address routine 1 – 20 repetitions (p 120)
Bunker play address routine 2 – 20 repetitions (p 122)
Bunker play 1 – 20 repetitions (p 124)
Bunker play 2 – 20 repetitions (p 125)
Putting address routine – 10 repetitions (p 126)
Putting stroke routine – 15 repetitions (p 127)
Short putts 1 – 20 repetitions (p 135)
Short putts 2 – 20 repetitions (p 136)

PITCHING AND BUNKER-PLAY REVIEW

Use the weekend to develop and refine your bunker-play skills so that you are able confidently to control the distance of your pitch shots and remove the ball from the sand first time every time.

ASSIGNMENTS

❶ Play a round and keep statistics on the key areas.

❷ Check your statistics against the performance-analysis table to identify any major weaknesses.

❸ Learn to play pitch shots with a variety of different clubs for extra versatility.

PRACTICE EXERCISES

Pitching 1 – 20 repetitions (p 108)
Pitching 2 – 20 repetitions (p 110)
Pitching 3 – 20 repetitions (p 111)
Pitching 4 – 10 repetitions (p 112)
Bunker play address routine 1 – 20 repetitions (p 120)
Bunker play address routine 2 – 20 repetitions (p 122)
Bunker play address routine 3 – 20 repetitions (p 123)
Bunker play 1 – 20 repetitions (p 124)
Bunker play 2 – 20 repetitions (p 125)
Putting address routine – 10 repetitions (p 126)
Putting stroke routine – 15 repetitions (p 127)
Short putts 1 – 20 repetitions (p 135)
Short putts 2 – 20 repetitions (p 136)

Short-game review

Now that you have practised all of the key individual areas of the short game, it is time to work on all of the elements together so that you have a total command of all the skills required to get up and down in two shots from around the green consistently.

YOUR SEVENTH WEEK
Although you will still be required to perform the recommended exercises prescribed by the performance-analysis table, during this week you will focus exclusively on all elements of the short game.

STRUCTURED PRACTICE
The practice routines that you will be performing this week will remind you of the techniques required to play the basic shots from within 60 yards of the green and will also help you improve your judgement of distance for ultimate control over every shot.

THIS WEEK'S PRIORITIES
Monday	The pitch shot
Tuesday	The chip shot
Wednesday	Bunker play
Thursday	Learning to improvise
Friday	Holing out
Weekend	Short-game focus

GOAL FOR THE WEEK
Your goal for this week is to improve your technique and enhance your sense of touch and feel in all of the key areas of the short game and to reach the required performance level to become a single-figure golfer.

THE PITCH SHOT

This is a key scoring area for golfers of all levels. The better players will be looking to get up and down in two shots from within 60 yards of the green, but it is also just as important to take no more than three shots to get the ball into the hole from this range. Ideally, the ball should finish no more than ten per cent of the original yardage away from the pin. For example, if your pitch shot is 60 yards long, you should look to land the ball within six yards of the hole.

ASSIGNMENTS

❶ Play a round and keep statistics on key areas.

❷ Check the performance-analysis table to identify any major weaknesses.

● Check your pitching yardages with all of your wedges and your backswing reference points.

❹ Practise varying the release through impact by either holding the clubface open through the ball or rotating your forearms more aggressively in order to produce shots with more spin that stop quickly and with less spin so that they release once they hit the green.

PRACTICE EXERCISES

Pitching 1 – 20 repetitions (p 108)
Pitching 2 – 20 repetitions (p 110)
Pitching 3 – 10 repetitions (p 111)
Pitching 4 – 20 repetitions (p 112)
Pitching 5 – 10 repetitions (p 113)
Pitching 6 – 10 repetitions (p 114)

THE BASIC CHIP SHOT

This is your stock shot around the green and you should be continually refining your technique and working on your touch and feel. If there are no obstacles between your ball and the hole, the shot is simply an extended version of your putting stroke and there is no reason why you cannot master the shot in a fairly short space of time. Develop your touch and ability to land the ball first bounce onto the green.

ASSIGNMENTS

❶ Hit 30 balls at the driving range, going through your address routine prior to hitting each shot.

❷ Work on your swing basics at home, ideally in front of a mirror.

❸ Experiment holding the club with your putting grip to play chip shots from the fringe. Reducing the wrist action helps keep the ball low to the ground.

❹ Practise landing the ball on the same spot on the green from the same position using a variety of different clubs.

PRACTICE EXERCISES

Chipping 1 – 20 repetitions (p 114)
Chipping 2 – 10 repetitions (p 116)
Chipping 3 – 10 repetitions (p 117)
Chipping feel 1 – 10 repetitions (p 118)
Chipping feel 2 – 20 repetitions (p 119)
Chipping feel 3 – 20 repetitions (p 120)

WEEK **7**

BUNKER PLAY

This is an area of the game that causes amateur golfers a lot of trouble. Do not feel pressurized into thinking that you have to get the ball up and down in two from the sand to become a low handicapper. If you can manage this 30 per cent of the time and hole out within three shots the rest of the time, your bunker play is more than adequate. Review the key changes you need to make to your set-up, understand why you need to make almost a full swing every time and strive to improve your technique and distance control.

ASSIGNMENTS

❶ Check your set-up and posture in front of a mirror and compare it with that of a top player with a similar build, using a golf magazine or an instruction book for reference.

❷ Practise your bunker-play set-up and get used to swinging along the line of your feet and body instead of along the ball/target line.

PRACTICE EXERCISES

Bunker play address routine 1 – 20 repetitions (p 120)

Bunker play address routine 2 – 20 repetitions (p 122)

Bunker play address routine 3 – 10 repetitions (p 123)

Bunker play 1 – 20 repetitions (p 124)

Bunker play 2 – 20 repetitions (p 125)

LEARNING TO IMPROVISE

You will frequently find your ball lying on bare ground, plugged in the sand or in the face of a bunker or even in a divot. An important part of becoming a single-figure golfer is being able to overcome these challenging situations and not allowing them to ruin your scores. Learn how to adapt your stance and amend your ball position, weight distribution, the angle of the clubface and even the swing to produce a wide variety of shots.

ASSIGNMENTS

❶ Work on the swing basics at home.

❷ Sit down and visualize yourself in the perfect set-up, making good swings, holing out confidently and accurately judging the pace of your putts.

❸ Take ten balls and throw them over your head around the practice chipping green and play each one as it lies.

PRACTICE EXERCISES

Chipping 1 – 20 repetitions (p 114)

Chipping 2 – 10 repetitions (p 116)

Chipping 3 – 10 repetitions (p 117)

Bunker play address routine 1 – 10 repetitions (p 120)

Bunker play address routine 2 – 10 repetitions (p 122)

Bunker play 1 – 10 repetitions (p 124)

Bunker play 2 – 10 repetitions (p 125)

Pitching 1 – 10 repetitions (p 108)

Pitching 2 – 10 repetitions (p 110)

Pitching 3 – 10 repetitions (p 111)

WEEK **7**

HOLING OUT WITH CONVICTION

Unfortunately, a deft chip, pitch or splash shot is only half the equation when it comes to getting up and down from off the green. In many instances, it is your ability to hole out from within six feet of the hole that determines the overall efficiency of your short game. Develop an authoritative and technically orthodox putting stroke that you can rely on to hit the target from within six feet.

ASSIGNMENTS

❶ Hit 50 balls at the driving range, going through the address routine before each and every shot.

❷ Watch a DVD of a golf tournament and see how the top professionals adhere to their pre-shot routines even under the severest pressure.

PRACTICE EXERCISES

Putting address routine – 10 repetitions (p 126)

Putting stroke routine – 15 repetitions (p 127)

Short putts 1 – 20 repetitions (p 135)

Short putts 2 – 20 repetitions (p 136)

Short putts 3 – 20 repetitions (p 137)

COMPLETE SHORT-GAME REVIEW

By now you should have a good understanding of all the components that combine to make up the short game. Aim for a success rate of 30–40 per cent from the sand, 50–60 per cent from around the green and 20–30 per cent from within 70 yards of the flag.

ASSIGNMENTS

❶ Play a round and keep statistics on the key areas.

❷ Check your statistics against the performance-analysis table to identify any major weaknesses.

❸ Ensure that you are using the same make and construction of ball for ultimate consistency.

PRACTICE EXERCISES

Pitching 1 – 20 repetitions (p 108)

Pitching 2 – 20 repetitions (p 110)

Pitching 3 – 20 repetitions (p 111)

Pitching 4 – 10 repetitions (p 112)

Bunker play address routine 1 – 20 repetitions (p 120)

Bunker play address routine 2 – 20 repetitions (p 122)

Bunker play 1 – 20 repetitions (p 124)

Bunker play 2 – 20 repetitions (p 125)

Putting address routine – 10 repetitions (p 126)

Putting stroke routine – 15 repetitions (p 127)

Short putts 1 – 20 repetitions (p 135)

Short putts 2 – 20 repetitions (p 136)

WEEK **7**

Learning how to score

Now that you have covered most of the major areas of the game, it is time to turn your attention away from the technical side of golf to the business of learning how to compile a good score. As any top professional will tell you, this is an art in itself and it is a crucial skill that you will have to learn if you are to achieve your goal of obtaining a single-figure handicap.

YOUR EIGHTH WEEK

This week you will be focusing primarily on developing your mental game and course-management skills. These are two vital areas of the game where you are capable of making instant improvements to your scoring simply by thinking in a more constructive and positive manner.

STRUCTURED PRACTICE

During this week you will concentrate more on playing than practising. Although you will still be required to perform the recommended practice exercises according to how your statistics compare with the performance-analysis table, most of the week will be spent learning how to prepare and think correctly on the course. During this week you should make it your goal to plan and think carefully about what you want to achieve with every shot you hit. Give yourself a specific outcome for each shot and see how close you come to achieving it.

THIS WEEK'S PRIORITIES

Monday	Developing a pre-round routine
Tuesday	Creating a game plan
Wednesday	Improving your mental game
Thursday	Basic percentage play
Friday	Playing the par-3s, par-4s and par-5s
Weekend	Putting it all together

WEEK 8

GOAL FOR THE WEEK

Your goal for this week is to learn how to minimize the number of mental/course-management errors that you make during a round and to avoid wasting shots unnecessarily out on the course.

DEVELOP A PRE-ROUND ROUTINE

The world's top players have a pre-round routine that they adhere to before every round of golf they play. This gives them a comfort zone and allows them to prepare in exactly the same way each time, leading to extra consistency. Develop your own pre-round routine that leaves you relaxed, ready and prepared for the opening tee shot and the round ahead.

ASSIGNMENTS

❶ Sit down and write a golf pre-round schedule starting from the moment you arrive at the course 45 minutes before your tee time. See advice on page 140 for how to structure your routine.

❷ Play a round of golf, adhering to your new pre-round schedule and keeping statistics on key areas of the game.

❸ Check the performance-analysis table to identify any major weaknesses.

PRACTICE EXERCISES

Pre-shot routine 1 – 10 repetitions (p 78)
Pre-shot routine 2 – 1 repetition (p 80)

DEVELOP A GAME PLAN FOR THE ROUND

If you play most of your golf at the same course, you should have a game plan for every hole in order to negotiate the round in the most efficient and effective manner. Even if you are playing a course for the first time, it is still a good idea to sit down before the round with a course planner and work out a strategy for the key holes in advance. Learn the importance of preparing for each round thoroughly and develop the habit of thinking about how you are going to play each hole and the course in advance.

ASSIGNMENTS

❶ Pretend that you are playing your home course at the driving range and select the clubs accordingly. Play each shot from where you believe it would have landed on the course itself until you reach the green.

❷ Continue to work on your basics at home and review your set-up in front of a mirror.

❸ Write down a game plan for your next round of golf at your home course.

❹ Check the stroke indexes on the card at your home course and ask yourself what makes the stroke index 1 hole the most difficult and stroke index 18 the easiest.

PRACTICE EXERCISES

Pre-shot routine 1 – 10 repetitions (p 78)
Pre-shot routine 2 – 1 repetition (p 80)

IMPROVING YOUR MENTAL GAME

From this point onwards in the plan, you need to be totally positive in your approach to the game. There is no room whatsoever for any negative thoughts or self-doubts and you should be focusing purely on achieving your single-figure handicap. Concentrate on the positive aspects of your game and the positive outcomes you are looking to achieve. Do not allow any negative thoughts to linger in your mind.

ASSIGNMENTS

❶ Visualize yourself in the perfect address position making the perfect swing.
❷ Hit 30 balls at the driving range, making sure you visualize each shot carefully before you play it.
❸ Reassess your goals. Are you still on target to achieve them or have you already done so? If so, you will need to set yourself new challenges.

PRACTICE EXERCISES

Pre-shot routine 1 – 10 repetitions (p 78)
Pre-shot routine 2 – 1 repetition (p 80)

BASIC PERCENTAGE PLAY

Now that you have greater control over your shot-making than at the beginning of the plan, improving your course management should not be too difficult. The principles remain the same, however, regardless of your skill level, although your strategies for playing certain holes will obviously change as your ability to play a wider variety of shots increases. Reassess your playing strategies so that they match your new skill level as a player.

ASSIGNMENTS

❶ Play a social round of golf, focusing purely on your course-management and visualization skills. Adhere to your game plan on every hole.
❷ Read the sections on course management and mental attitude to remind yourself of the key principles.
❸ After your round, reflect only on the good shots that you played and visualize them clearly in your mind.

PRACTICE EXERCISES

Pre-shot routine 1 – 10 repetitions (p 78)
Pre-shot routine 2 – 1 repetition (p 80)

PLAYING STRATEGIES FOR DIFFERENT HOLES

By now you should have a good idea of your relative strengths and weaknesses in all areas of the game. You can use this information to determine your playing strategies for different types of holes, such as long and short par-3s, par-4s and par-5s. Identify the key strengths and weaknesses in your game and plan your game and your playing strategies around them. The aim is to maximize the number of shots you play using your favourite club and minimize the number of shots played with your least favourite club or from your least favourite yardage or position.

ASSIGNMENTS

❶ Take just your least favourite club to the range and hit as many balls as it takes for you to restore your confidence.

❷ Sit down and think about the playing characteristics of your own course and identify the key shots that you need to be able to play on the par-3s, par-4s and par-5s to shoot a good score.

❸ Watch a DVD of a golf tournament and see how the top professionals negotiate the toughest holes.

PRACTICE EXERCISES

Pre-shot routine 1 – 10 repetitions (p 78)
Pre-shot routine 2 – 1 repetition (p 80)

COMBINING YOUR KEY COURSE-MANAGEMENT SKILLS

Good attitude, preparation and decision-making combine to form good course management. Your focus for the weekend is to develop your key pre-round and address routines so that they incorporate good visualization and planning skills. This will help you maintain a high level of concentration so that you minimize the chances of making mental errors on the golf course.

ASSIGNMENTS

❶ Play a round of golf and keep statistics on the key areas.

❷ Check your statistics against the performance-analysis table to identify any major weaknesses and perform the relevant exercises.

❸ Hit 50 balls at the driving range, going through your address routine before each shot.

PRACTICE EXERCISES

Pre-shot routine 1 – 10 repetitions (p 78)
Pre-shot routine 2 – 1 repetition (p 80)

WEEK **8**

Refining the key score-saving areas

Heading into the last couple of weeks of your golf-improvement plan, your focus should be on tightening up all areas of your game so that there are no obvious weaknesses, and polishing all the techniques you will require in the key scoring areas of the game.

YOUR NINTH WEEK
During your ninth week, you will refine the key scoring areas of the game such as your driving, iron play, long-range putting, pitching and chipping.

STRUCTURED PRACTICE
The practice routines that you will be performing this week will enable you to improve your performance in all of the areas of the game that traditionally cause amateur golfers the most problems and which lead to dropped shots.

THIS WEEK'S PRIORITIES

Monday	Driving
Tuesday	Distance control with irons
Wednesday	Pitching
Thursday	Chipping
Friday	Long-range putting
Weekend	Weekly review

GOAL FOR THE WEEK
Your goal for this week is to maximize your scoring potential in all of the key areas of the game.

DRIVING

In order to play to single figures, you will need to be able to drive the ball over 200 yards off the tee with a good degree of accuracy regularly. This will enable you to reach the shorter par-4s with your second shot and also give you a good chance of either hitting the greens on longer par-4s in regulation or, at worst, leaving yourself a pitch or chip for your third shot. The longer and straighter you can drive the ball, the easier the rest of the hole becomes.

ASSIGNMENTS

❶ Play a round of golf, keeping statistics on key areas of the game.

❷ Check the performance-analysis table to identify any major weaknesses.

❸ Pick out small targets to aim at when driving off the tee to minimize your margin for error.

PRACTICE EXERCISES

Alignment 1 – 10 repetitions (p 80)
Alignment 2 – 10 repetitions (p 82)
Alignment 3 – 10 repetitions (p 83)
Ball position 1 – 10 repetitions (p 87)
Posture 2 – 5 repetitions (p 85)
Driver set-up – 10 repetitions (p 99)
Driver swing – 10 repetitions (p 100)
Driver backswing – 10 repetitions (p 102)

CONTROLLING DISTANCE WITH IRONS

Many shots are dropped as a result of failing to reach the green with an approach shot. These are needless errors and are normally caused by not knowing how far you hit the ball with each club and/or allowing your ego to get in the way of your club selection. Eliminate the causes of under-clubbing from your game by measuring your yardages with each club and becoming more disciplined in your club selection and more realistic in your perception of how far you can hit the ball.

ASSIGNMENTS

❶ Work out your yardages with each club in the bag.

❷ Hit five balls with each club at the range and ask yourself how many shots you hit perfectly.

❸ Continue to work on your basics at home. Your grip and posture are particularly important for good ball-striking.

PRACTICE EXERCISES

Alignment 1 – 10 repetitions (p 80)
Alignment 2 – 10 repetitions (p 82)
Alignment 3 – 10 repetitions (p 83)
Posture 1 – 10 repetitions (p 84)
Posture 2 – 5 repetitions (p 85)
Ball position 2 – 10 repetitions (p 88)
Swing drill 1 – 10 repetitions (p 90)
Swing drill 2 – 10 repetitions (p 91)
Swing drill 3 – 10 repetitions (p 93)
Swing drill 4 – 10 repetitions (p 94)

PITCHING

The number of pitch shots that you hit during an average round of golf is a good barometer of the overall quality of your game. If you continually have to pitch onto the green from within 30 to 70 yards, your long game clearly isn't good enough. However, this is still a key scoring area of the game because you will probably encounter several pitch shots on par-5s and long par-4s. Develop your pitching technique and distance control so that you can consistently land the ball on the green and close to the flag.

ASSIGNMENTS

❶ Measure your pitching yardages with all your wedges and make a note of how far you hit the ball with various lengths of backswing.

❷ Experiment with the ball position, clubface angle at address and the release through impact to produce shots of differing trajectories and with varying amounts of spin.

PRACTICE EXERCISES

Pitching 1 – 20 repetitions (p 108)
Pitching 2 – 20 repetitions (p 110)
Pitching 3 – 20 repetitions (p 111)
Pitching 4 – 10 repetitions (p 112)
Grip 1 – 10 repetitions (p 74)
Grip 2 – 10 repetitions (p 75)
Posture 1 – 20 repetitions (p 84)
Posture 2 – 20 repetitions (p 85)

CHIPPING

The most common amateur mistake is keeping the same width of stance and ball position for every shot regardless of whether you are hitting a driver or a pitching wedge. Strive to improve your basic technique and distance control and develop more versatility around the greens.

ASSIGNMENTS

❶ Hit 30 shots at the range, going through a full address routine before each shot.

❷ Practise chipping, using a variety of clubs to improve feel and versatility.

❸ Watch a DVD of a golf tournament and see how the top players keep the ball low to the ground wherever possible around the greens.

PRACTICE EXERCISES

Chipping 1 – 50 repetitions (p 114)
Chipping 2 – 30 repetitions (p 116)
Chipping 3 – 20 repetitions (p 117)
Chipping feel 1 – 20 repetitions (p 118)
Chipping feel 2 – 20 repetitions (p 119)
Chipping feel 3 – 20 repetitions (p 120)
Short putts 1 – 20 repetitions (p 135)
Short putts 2 – 20 repetitions (p 136)

LONG-RANGE PUTTING

Three-putting from long range is probably the most common cause of dropped shots. In most cases, it is due to poor judgement of the approach putt and, more often than not, the main error is leaving the ball well short of the hole. If you can eliminate such a hesitant approach from your putting, your scores will fall rapidly.

ASSIGNMENT

❶ Work on your putting indoors. Hitting practice putts across a carpet is a good way to train yourself to make a more positive strike.

PRACTICE EXERCISES
Reading greens 1 – 15 repetitions (p 130)
Putting address routine – 15 repetitions (p 126)
Putting technique 2 – 5 repetitions (p 131)
Putting stroke routine – 10 repetitions (p 127)
Putting technique 1 – 15 repetitions (p 129)
Putting feel 1 – 15 repetitions (p 132)
Putting feel 2 – 15 repetitions (p 133)
Putting feel 3 – 15 repetitions (p 134)

WEEKLY REVIEW

Improving consistency in all of the key scoring areas of the game is vital for shooting lower scores and for eliminating wasted shots.

ASSIGNMENT

❶ Play a round and keep statistics on the key areas. Check your statistics against the performance-analysis table to identify any major weaknesses.

PRACTICE EXERCISES
Driver set-up – 10 repetitions (p 99)
Driver swing – 10 repetitions (p 100)
Pitching 1 – 20 repetitions (p 108)
Pitching 2 – 20 repetitions (p 110)
Grip 1 – 10 repetitions (p 74)
Grip 2 – 10 repetitions (p 75)
Chipping 1 – 50 repetitions (p 114)
Chipping 2 – 30 repetitions (p 116)
Chipping feel 1 – 20 repetitions (p 118)
Chipping feel 2 – 20 repetitions (p 119)
Short putts 1 – 20 repetitions (p 135)
Short putts 2 – 20 repetitions (p 136)
Putting technique 2 – 5 repetitions (p 131)
Putting stroke routine – 10 repetitions (p 127)
Putting feel 1 – 15 repetitions (p 132)
Putting feel 2 – 15 repetitions (p 133)

WEEK
9

WEEK 10 ▶ ## Review and refine your skills

By this stage in the plan, you should have reached a level where you are at least competent in all areas of the game and hopefully only minor adjustments will now be needed in order for you to reach the standard required to become a single-figure golfer.

YOUR TENTH WEEK

In this last week you will be fine-tuning all areas of your game so that there are no obvious weaknesses that will let you down on the golf course. You will be reviewing and fine-tuning your techniques and routines so that you can play to your full potential. You will also be asked to play more regularly during the week in order to sharpen up your scoring ability on the course. This is also your final opportunity to iron out any possible weaknesses in your game so that you are confident of dealing with any situation that may arise out on the golf course.

STRUCTURED PRACTICE

You will already have performed all of the practice exercises at various stages during the preceding ten weeks. However, during the final seven days of the plan you will need to repeat many of these drills and routines in order to refresh your memory and get accustomed to specific techniques and preparation.

THIS WEEK'S PRIORITIES

Monday	Basics refresher course
Tuesday	The swing
Wednesday	The long game
Thursday	The short game
Friday	Putting
Weekend	Intensive practice

GOAL FOR THE WEEK

Your goal for this week is simply to ensure that every single part of your game, including your mental approach and course management, reaches the standard required in the performance-analysis table.

WEEK 10

BASICS REFRESHER COURSE

For the last ten weeks, you should have been continually working on the fundamentals and developing your pre-shot routine. But, it is easy for bad habits to creep in, so now's the time to ensure that your grip, stance, alignment and posture are all in good shape so that you maximize your chances of adopting the correct address position.

FINE-TUNING YOUR SWING

Building on the established foundations of a good grip, stance, alignment and posture, reacquaint yourself with the correct body pivot, arm swing, wrist action and resistance that combine to create a solid and repetitive swing. Rehearse the key elements of the golf swing so that they blend together to form a free-flowing, continuous motion.

ASSIGNMENTS

❶ Check the quality of your address position in a mirror so that you can monitor your alignment and posture.

❷ Re-read the section on improving your mental approach to the game.

❸ Play nine holes of golf without analyzing your score or recording any statistics.

PRACTICE EXERCISES

Grip 1 – 10 repetitions (p 74)

Grip 2 – 5 repetitions (p 75)

Grip 3 – 5 repetitions (p 76)

Pre-shot routine 1 – 10 repetitions (p 78)

Alignment 1 – 10 repetitions (p 80)

Alignment 2 – 10 repetitions (p 82)

Posture 1 – 10 repetitions (p 84)

Posture 2 – 10 repetitions (p 85)

Posture 3 – 1 repetition (p 86)

Ball position 1 – 5 repetitions (p 87)

Ball position 2 – 5 repetitions (p 88)

Ball position 3 – 5 repetitions (p 89)

ASSIGNMENTS

❶ Re-read the section on The Swing – Week 2 of the plan.

❷ Make plenty of practice swings without a ball in front of a mirror, focusing on the key checkpoints of the takeaway, halfway back and top of the backswing.

❸ Visit the driving range and hit 30 balls, adhering to your address routine on each shot and performing one key swing exercise before hitting each ball.

PRACTICE EXERCISES

Swing drill 1 – 15 repetitions (p 90)

Swing drill 2 – 15 repetitions (p 91)

Swing drill 3 – 10 repetitions (p 93)

Swing drill 4 – 10 repetitions (p 94)

Swing tempo 1 – 10 repetitions (p 96)

Swing tempo 2 – 10 repetitions (p 97)

Swing tempo 3 – 5 repetitions (p 98)

THE LONG GAME

Review your driving/fairway wood play and your ball-striking with your irons. Practise hitting different trajectories of shots until you are confident in your ability to shape the ball at will and are versatile enough to deal with any situation out on the course. Remember that you are looking for a general level of consistency so you hit the fairway more often and hit around 50 per cent of the greens in regulation.

ASSIGNMENTS

❶ Note your yardages by hitting ten balls with each club. Ignore the best and worst two shots and take an average yardage of the remaining six balls.

❷ Re-read the section on course management and play nine holes of golf without analyzing your score or recording statistics.

❸ Review the make-up of your set. Are there any clubs that you should substitute – such as a long iron for a fairway wood.

PRACTICE EXERCISES

Driver set-up – 10 repetitions (p 99)
Driver swing – 10 repetitions (p 100)
Driver backswing – 5 repetitions (p 102)
Shaping shots 1 – 10 repetitions (p 102)
Shaping shots 2 – 10 repetitions (p 104)
Shaping shots 3 – 10 repetitions (p 105)
Trajectory 1 – 10 repetitions (p 106)
Trajectory 2 – 10 repetitions (p 107)
Trajectory 3 – 10 repetitions (p 108)

SHORT-GAME REVIEW

Placing the ball close to the hole can help cancel out previous errors, so you should work on touch and feel around the greens, aiming to achieve a high level of consistency.

ASSIGNMENTS

❶ Play with a friend of a similar standard and turn the practice session into a series of competitions.

❷ Hit a pitch shot with different wedges and see how far you hit the ball with each club. Note how the distance changes when swinging from hip, chest and shoulder height. Also, change the angle of the clubface at address to see how to get different heights and distances.

PRACTICE EXERCISES

Pitching 1 – 20 repetitions (p 108)
Pitching 2 – 10 repetitions (p 110)
Pitching 3 – 10 repetitions (p 111)
Pitching 4 – 10 repetitions (p 112)
Chipping 1 – 20 repetitions (p 114)
Chipping 2 – 10 repetitions (p 116)
Chipping 3 – 10 repetitions (p 117)
Chipping feel 1 – 10 repetitions (p 118)
Chipping feel 2 – 10 repetitions (p 119)
Chipping feel 3 – 10 repetitions (p 120)
Bunker play address routine 1 –
　5 repetitions (p 120)
Bunker play address routine 2 –
　10 repetitions (p 122)
Bunker play 1 – 10 repetitions (p 124)
Bunker play 2 – 5 repetitions (p 125)

PUTTING

The ability to hole putts consistently can more than make up for deficiencies in the long game. The key skill to learn is distance control from long range. Review your putting address position and work on developing the quality of your putting stroke, concentrating especially on keeping your head and lower body steady.

ASSIGNMENTS

❶ Rehearse and refine your green-reading routine so that it becomes second nature and consistent.

❷ Watch a DVD of a golf tournament and see how closely your pre-putt routine resembles those of the top players.

PRACTICE EXERCISES

Putting address routine – 15 repetitions (p 126)

Putting stroke routine – 20 repetitions (p 127)

Putting posture – 5 repetitions (p 128)

Putting technique 1 – 10 repetitions (p 129)

Putting technique 2 – 10 repetitions (p 131)

Reading greens – 10 repetitions (p 130)

Putting feel 1 – 20 repetitions (p 132)

Putting feel 2 – 10 repetitions (p 133)

Putting feel 3 – 10 repetitions (p 134)

Short putts 1 – 10 repetitions (p 135)

Short putts 2 – 10 repetitions (p 136)

Short putts 3 – 10 repetitions (p 137)

INTENSIVE PRACTICE

This is your last chance to iron out any lingering glitches, so spend the whole weekend reviewing each of the key areas of your game. Start with one final review of your fundamentals and resist the temptation to make major amendments to your technique and instead focus on fine-tuning all areas of your game. Target your remaining weaknesses to ensure that you are competent in every department. You should aim to reach a level where you are confident in your ability to play every shot.

ASSIGNMENTS

❶ Develop a game plan for your next round of golf and make sure that you stick to it regardless of how tempted you might be to change your strategy.

❷ Play a round of golf adhering to your routines and adopting all of the mental game and course-management skills and principles outlined in the first section of the book.

PRACTICE EXERCISES

Perform as many repetitions as possible of all the recommended practice routines and exercises. Continue to focus on the weakest parts of your game until you are satisfied that they are of the required standard.

WEEK
10

OVERVIEW OF YOUR 10-WEEK PLAN

WEEK 1
- Mon — Building a neutral grip
- Tues — Posture
- Wed — Stance and ball position
- Thur — Alignment
- Fri — The address routine
- W/E — Putting it all together

WEEK 2
- Mon — The upper body pivot
- Tues — The swinging of the arms
- Wed — How and when to hinge your wrists
- Thur — The role of the lower body
- Fri — Developing good rhythm
- W/E — Restoring the spontaneity

WEEK 3
- Mon — Refining your putting set-up
- Tues — Developing the putting stroke
- Wed — Learning to read greens
- Thur — Controlling the distance of putts
- Fri — Holing out from short range
- W/E — Putting it all together

WEEK 4
- Mon — Chipping set-up
- Tues — Chipping technique
- Wed — Chipping distance control
- Thur — Improving your imagination
- Fri — Holing the pressure putts
- W/E — Consolidating the week's activities

WEEK 5
- Mon — Driving and fairway woods
- Tues — Long and short irons
- Wed — Fade shots
- Thur — Draw shots
- Fri — High shots and low shots
- W/E — Refining your shot-making skills

WEEK 6
- Mon — Pitching – the basic technique
- Tues — Pitching – judging distance
- Wed — Bunker play – the set-up
- Thur — Bunker play – the swing
- Fri — Holing out
- W/E — A review of the week's work

WEEK 7
- Mon — The pitch shot
- Tues — The chip shot
- Wed — Bunker play
- Thur — Learning to improvise
- Fri — Holing out
- W/E — Short-game focus

WEEK 8
- Mon — Developing a pre-round routine
- Tues — Creating a game plan
- Wed — Improving your mental game
- Thur — Basic percentage play
- Fri — Playing the par-3s, par-4s and par-5s
- W/E — Putting it all together

WEEK 9
- Mon — Driving
- Tues — Distance control with irons
- Wed — Pitching
- Thur — Chipping
- Fri — Long-range putting
- W/E — Weekly review

WEEK 10
- Mon — Basics refresher course
- Tues — The swing
- Wed — The long game
- Thur — The short game
- Fri — Putting
- W/E — Intensive practice

WEEK 1 2 3 4 5 6 7 8 9 10

This section includes all of the practice exercises and routines that you will need to elevate each area of your game to the standard required to become a single-figure golfer. The exercises are not always designed to give you the perfect technique, but are aimed to help you eliminate your problem areas quickly so that you can avoid the disaster shots that ruin so many promising rounds.

It is important to remember that the exercises – particularly those where you are looking to improve key areas of your technique – are dependent on you assuming the correct address position in the first place. There is little point, for example, in trying to improve your shoulder turn if your posture is slumped and your spine angle is curved, because if that is the case the exercise simply will not work.

Finally, always remember that quality is far better than quantity when it comes to practice. If you are pushed for time on a particular day, it is far better to do fewer repetitions and retain good form and focus than to rush through the exercises without taking the time to prepare properly. You can always catch up the following day – just as long as you do not make a habit of it!

GRIP EXERCISE 1

forming a neutral grip

The way in which you place your hands on the club influences many other aspects of your swing. Although a text-book grip is not absolutely essential for playing good golf, it will maximize your chances of squaring the clubface at impact to achieve both power and accuracy. This is why it is worth making a concentrated effort to get it right.

1 Allow your arms to hang by your sides so that your forearms and palms turn in slightly towards your thighs. If you look down at your hands, this is how they should look when they are placed on the club.

2 Keeping your left arm by your side, slot the grip of the club into the fingers of your left hand. Make sure that your forearm maintains its shape and that you do not rotate your hand as you do this.

3 Bring your right arm across, making sure that your forearm and palm remain turned inwards slightly. Place your right hand on the club, holding the grip at the base of your fingers. This is now a natural and neutral grip.

GRIP EXERCISE 2

establishing the correct grip pressure

While the formation of the grip is very important, exactly how tightly you should hold the club is a factor that is often overlooked.

1 Hold a 7-iron out in front of you so that it is horizontal to the ground. In this position the club should feel very heavy and you will have to grip the club tightly to prevent it from falling to the ground.

2 This time hold your 7-iron in front of you upright and directly above your hands. In this position the clubhead will feel very light and your grip pressure will be too loose.

3 Finally, hold your 7-iron out in front of you so that it is tilted away from you at a 45-degree angle. The amount of pressure your hands need to apply to the club to hold it in position without allowing it to fall is the correct pressure for all normal shots.

GRIP EXERCISE 3

strengthening your hands

If you have good strength in your hands and wrists you will have more control over the club when you swing and you will be able to create more power.

1 Extend your left arm gently out in front of you and hold the club in the base of your fingers so that it hangs vertically.

2 Without moving your arm, work the grip of the club upwards through your hands using only your fingers.

3 After reaching the end of the grip, work it back down again and repeat the process.

GRIP EXERCISE 4

work on your grip at home

You do not have to do this at the range, it is possible to do this exercise wherever you are.

1 Make sure that you have a club close at hand whenever possible.

2 Work on your grip at any time, even while watching the television.

3 Practise forming your new grip as much as possible during the first few days of the plan so that it becomes both a natural and comfortable procedure.

PRE-SHOT ROUTINE EXERCISE 1

key components of your routine

Every top golfer has a pre-shot routine that they go through prior to hitting each shot on the golf course. A routine gives you a comfort zone and also maximizes your chances of setting up correctly each time. Your own routine will be personal to you, but here are the key elements that it should include:

1 Start by visualizing the shot you want to hit while standing several feet behind the ball facing the target. Picture the shape and trajectory of the shot.

2 Walk into the ball from the left side. Look at your intended line and keep your chest facing the target until you begin to step in to form your stance.

3 Set the clubface carefully behind the ball so that it is aiming where you want it to go. Constantly refer to the target with your eyes so that you are certain that you are aligned correctly.

4 Finally, taking your lead from the clubface, position your body and feet so that they are square to the target line. Now you should be in the perfect position to hit your shot.

PRE-SHOT ROUTINE EXERCISE 2

time your routine for ultimate consistency

Your ultimate goal is to practise and rehearse your pre-shot routine so that it is exactly the same each time you address the ball.

1 Take the club out of the bag and set up to strike the ball.

2 Make sure that the amount of time you take does not vary by more than a second or so on any pre-shot routine.

3 Ask a friend to time your pre-shot routine for you.

ALIGNMENT EXERCISE 1

aim the clubface before the body

If you watch any top player on television, one of the things that you will notice is that they always aim the clubface at their intended target before they complete their stance. This is because it is easier to see where the club is aiming before you stand side-on to the target.

1 First, stand behind the ball and visualize the shot you want to hit. Pick out an intermediate target a few feet in front of the ball on your intended line so that you can align the clubface more accurately.

2 Keeping your chest facing the target, place the clubface behind the ball with your right hand. Check that the clubface is aimed correctly by looking up and down the line between your ball and the target.

3 Finally, place your feet squarely to the leading edge of the clubface and ensure that the alignment of your feet and shoulders take their lead from the clubface, not the other way round.

ALIGNMENT EXERCISE 2

instinctive parallel alignment

Whenever you practise it is always a good idea to place a couple of shafts on the ground square to your target line so that you are aligned correctly before you hit a ball. If you repeat the exercise regularly enough, good alignment will become a natural and instinctive part of your pre-shot preparation.

1 Reinforce the message that the clubface and your body are aligned squarely to each other, but not aiming at the same point, by laying a shaft on the ground just outside the ball. Lay another shaft on the ground parallel to the first along the line of your feet. The ball should be roughly in the centre between the two shafts.

2 Once your body and the clubface are aligned squarely to each other, you have a much better chance of starting the swing on the correct path and plane. Hit every practice shot from the same set-up to improve your consistency and give you better feedback on the quality of your game.

ALIGNMENT EXERCISE 3

check shoulder aim

An excellent way of checking to see if you are aligned correctly at address is to take your normal stance and then lift your left arm straight up to the side of you. Ideally, your arm should point parallel left of your intended target. If it points at, or right of, your target, your shoulders are too closed. If your arm points too far left of the target, your shoulders are too open.

POSTURE EXERCISE 1

build your grip and tilt from hip

The most common and damaging posture flaw is simply setting down at address without making an effort to tilt forwards. This prevents you from creating a good spine angle to coil around during the swing and reduces both your power and your consistency.

1 Hold the club out in front of you at approximately chest height. Make sure that both arms are gently extended –

neither excessively straight nor bent and jammed in against your chest. Lower the club towards the ground by tilting forwards from your hips so that your bottom begins to stick out and your legs start to straighten.

2 When the clubhead reaches the ground, flex your knees gently so that you remove the tension from your legs, but do not lose any height. Now you are in the perfect address position.

1   2

POSTURE EXERCISE 2

match posture to the club

Although you can use exactly the same routine to create your posture with every club in the bag, the different lengths of shaft in the clubs will mean that you need to stand nearer to the ball with your wedges than with your fairway woods and driver. Consequently, you will need to tilt forwards at address more to reach the grip of your pitching wedge than your driver, where your posture will automatically be a little more upright. Get used to the different postures required for the different clubs.

1 *Driver* – Take the club and stand further away from the ball to compensate for the extra length of this club. Check that your posture is a little more upright than with your irons.

2 *Pitching wedge* – Take the club and place your feet nearer the ball. Tilt your upper body forward to reach the grip. Make sure that you compensate for the shorter and steeper shaft of the club.

1   2

POSTURE EXERCISE 3

your posture quality-control test

You should carry out this exercise on a regular basis as it will help you to correct your posture and, later on, it will stop you slipping back into any bad habits.

1 Check the quality of your posture by hanging a club straight down from your shoulders.

2 Create the correct angles at address by ensuring that the club points vertically down in line with the front of your knees and the balls of your feet. If the club hangs inside your knees, correct your posture by tilting from your hips instead of simply sitting on your heels to lower yourself to the ball.

BALL POSITION EXERCISE 1

setting up for the driver

Your feet, legs and hips form a solid base for a powerful swing.

1 Stand with your feet together and with the ball directly in the centre and your weight evenly balanced.

2 Take a very small step to the left with your left foot followed by a much larger one to the right with your right foot.

3 Check that you have placed yourself in the correct position for hitting a driver or fairway wood before you start making the shot.

BALL POSITION EXERCISE 2

setting up for the short irons

The set-up for irons is different from the driver because the ball is played further back in the stance.

1 Stand with your feet together and with the ball directly in the centre and your weight evenly balanced.

2 Take a slightly larger step to the left with your left foot than for the driver followed by one exactly the same length to the right with your right foot. This should place the ball dead centre in your stance – perfect for your short irons and wedges.

1

2

BALL POSITION EXERCISE 3

build ball position into your routine

Here's a simple driving range exercise to help you achieve perfect ball position.

1 Place a club on the ground in line with the target between the ball and your toes. Place the ball where you usually position it for the club you are using.

2 Place another club perpendicular to the other in line with the ball. This will give you reference for where the ball was in your stance once it's been hit.

3 Hit a number of range balls, repositioning each one in your stance until you are hitting straight shots.

SWING DRILL 1

the pivot trainer

This is the ultimate swing-building exercise and is used by the world's top golf coaches to develop the correct coiling motion of the upper body in the swing. This exercise only works if you have a good posture.

upper body until the shaft of the club points directly in front of you. Retain your spine angle from address and see your right knee has remained flexed. Resist the coiling motion with your lower body and keep your right knee as still as possible as you turn your shoulders.

1 Adopt your normal golfing posture. Hold a club just below your shoulders, with arms crossed across your chest to hold it in place.

2 Maintaining both your spine angle and the flex in your right knee, turn your

3 Turn your shoulders back the other way, again maintaining the angle in your spine and your knee flex. Hold these angles until the clubshaft is pointing directly out in front of you again. Once past the point of impact, allow your spine to straighten as you simulate the end of the swing by rotating your chest towards the target.

1   2   3

SWING DRILL 2

train your downswing

The most important area of the swing to get right is the area from waist height in the downswing to waist height in the follow-through, since this is when the clubhead is delivered to the ball and released through the point of impact.

1 Starting from your address position, swing the club away smoothly until your hands reach hip height. At this stage in the swing, the clubshaft should be square to the target line and parallel to the ground. The toe of the club should point straight up in the air.

2 Swing back down again and into your follow-through until your hands once again reach hip height. The clubshaft should be parallel to the ground and square to the target line and, once again, the toe of the club should point straight up in the air.

PRACTICE SWING DRILL

swing hands in backswing and follow-through

Making practice swings will help you to develop a feel for a good swing.

1 Swing your hands into a position where they are above your right shoulder at the top of the backswing and then above your left shoulder in the follow-through.

2 Watch how your arms swing up and down as your body rotates during the swing and how your wrists hinge in the backswing.

3 Release at impact and then re-hinge in the follow-through.

SWING DRILL 3

the pre-set drill

Many golfers are confused about how and when they should hinge their wrists in the backswing. This exercise enables you to feel how the wrists hinge the club in the backswing to create power and achieve the correct plane.

1 Holding a 7-iron, stand at address with your normal golf posture. Focus on keeping your lower back nice and straight, since good posture is crucial for this exercise.

2 Without moving or lifting your hands, hinge your wrists upwards so that the clubhead raises off the ground into the air. Stop when your wrists cannot hinge any further.

3 With your wrists set in this position, complete your swing by turning your shoulders around your spine angle in the backswing.

SWING DRILL 4

set the right wrist back

This exercise demonstrates how the right wrist, as well as hingeing upwards in the swing, also sets back on itself.

1 Holding a mid-iron in your hand, address the ball with your normal posture.

2 Hinge your right wrist back so that the shaft of the club is parallel to the target line and horizontal to the ground.

3 Now simply turn your shoulders and swing your arms up in the air to complete your backswing.

1

2

3

ANGLE DRILL

the clubface angle

The angle that you hit the ball at can make the difference between a straight shot or a sliced or hooked shot.

1 Keep your grip neutral and hinge your wrists correctly during the backswing.

2 Make sure that the clubface is hanging at a 45-degree angle to the ground.

3 Check that the toe of the club is not pointing straight down, as the clubface will be too open and this will lead to sliced or pushed shots.

4 Ensure that the grooves don't face the sky, as the clubface will be too closed, leading to off-line shots.

SWING TEMPO EXERCISE 1

the machine-gun drill

In this exercise, do not worry where the balls go. The key is to stay continually moving so that you do not have time to think about anything when standing over the ball.

1 Tee up several balls in a row, set yourself up to the first ball and relax your grip pressure.

2 Hit the first ball away and then step forward to the next in the line and immediately start your backswing.

3 Work your way through the entire row of balls without pausing in between shots.

SWING TEMPO EXERCISE 2

give your swing a head start

Most swing tempo problems originate from a lack of rhythm and fluidity in the takeaway where the club is propelled into motion from a stationary position. This exercise removes the first potential awkward few feet of the backswing, thereby improving the pace and rhythm of your whole swing.

1 Address the ball normally with a mid-iron and then swing the club a few feet forwards toward the target.

2 Without stopping, swing the club back and into your full backswing. You do not need to think of anything technical. Simply allow the momentum of the club to help you complete your swing.

SWING TEMPO EXERCISE 3

right-handed swings

A quick swing is normally dominated by the left side of the body approaching impact. You should hone this with the following exercise.

Free your right side by making some one-handed swings holding the club with just your right hand.

Perform this exercise one-handed several times then recreate the same feelings in your real swing.

Being able to maintain a steady swing tempo when under pressure is a great asset to all golfers. Watch Ernie Els, Vijay Singh or Retief Goosen when they are in contention for first place in a tournament. They retain their tempo and rhythm on every shot. If you have the opportunity, watch players like these on the practice range before they play their rounds. Much of their practice is focused on swing tempo and rhythm, getting the body and muscles to remember that tempo, to be able to recreate it reliably in the heat of battle – and all three of them hit the ball prodigious distances with their seemingly effortless swings.

DRIVER SET-UP EXERCISE

The driver is the longest and least forgiving club in the bag, which is why you need a perfect set-up if you want to get the full potential out of this important piece of equipment.

A good image to hold in your mind when practising your driver set-up is that of a reverse 'K'. Form your left arm and the club shaft into the straight line which will act as a lever to apply maximum pressure to the ball at impact, while your right arm and right leg form the spokes of the letter.

Stand more upright than when hitting a short iron. Make sure that your feet and shoulders are aimed squarely to the target, since the lack of loft on the clubface will accentuate any flaws at address. Such a wide swing demands a firm stance.

DRIVER SWING EXERCISE

Modern metal woods are far more forgiving than old wooden drivers, but a consistent swing is still required to take maximum advantage of the extra length produced by modern drivers.

1 Stand with your feet approximately shoulder-width apart to give yourself a solid base. Make sure that your left arm and the club form a straight line and that your weight favours your right side by about 60:40. Play the ball just under your left armpit.

2 Swing the club away smoothly through a wide arc. Ideally the shaft of the club should reach a position where it is horizontal to the ground at the top of the backswing.

3 Ensure that the transition between backswing and downswing is as smooth as possible. Do not lunge at the ball with your upper body to create distance. Swing your arms down in front of your body and keep your head behind the ball at impact.

4 To create maximum power it is essential that your weight is moving forwards towards the target at the point of impact. Finish with your weight on your front foot and your chest facing the target.

DRIVER BACKSWING EXERCISE

rehearse a low, sweeping takeaway

For many golfers there is often a temptation to start the swing too quickly when hitting the driver. To prevent this you should practise this exercise.

1 Constantly rehearse your takeaway, gliding the club smoothly away from the ball to create the wide swing arc that is necessary to produce both the power and the distance.

2 Keep the clubhead low to the ground for the first couple of feet of the takeaway, but do not force the club down once the momentum of the swing and your wrist hinge have taken effect.

SHAPING SHOTS EXERCISE 1

the fade shot

To hit a fade shot – curving the ball from left to right in the air – the clubface must be slightly open (that is, aiming right) to the path of the swing at the point of impact, so that it cuts across the ball imparting a left-to-right spin.

1 Whichever way you wish to curve the ball, always start by aiming the clubface at your intended target. Once you have done this, align your feet, hips and shoulders slightly to the left.

2 Swing the club away along the line of your feet and body, not along the target line. This will feel as though you are going to hit the ball to the left.

3 Swing back down to the ball on the same path – along the line of your feet. Although you are swinging to the left, the clubface will aim at your intended target at impact.

4 Ensure that your swing path conflicts with the clubface to produce the curved (left to right) ball flight.

SHAPING SHOTS EXERCISE 2

the draw

To hit a draw – curving the ball from right to left in the air – the clubface must be slightly closed (that is, aiming left) to the path of the swing at the point of impact, so that it cuts across the ball imparting a right-to-left spin in a similar way to how a tennis player hits a forehand topspin passing shot.

1 As with the fade, start by aiming the clubface at your intended target. Once you have done this, align your feet, hips and shoulders slightly to the right.

2 Swing the club away along the line of your feet and body, not along the target line. This will feel as though you are going to hit the ball to the right.

3 Swing back down to the ball on the same path – along the line of your feet. Although you are swinging to the right, the clubface will aim at your intended target at impact. Your swing path conflicts with the clubface to produce the curved (right to left) ball flight.

SHAPING SHOTS EXERCISE 3

vary your forearm release

By setting up either open or closed to the target to hit a fade or a draw, you can accentuate the movement by the way in which you release your forearms through the ball.

1 To hit a fade, feel as though your left forearm remains above the right as you strike the ball.

2 To hit a draw, allow your right forearm to rotate over the left through the ball.

TRAJECTORY EXERCISE 1

high shots

The ability to vary the trajectory of your shots will help you become a more versatile player. The secret to hitting shots of different heights is altering your ball position and either reducing or increasing the amount of wrist action in your swing.

To hit a high shot, your wrists need to be active during the swing to create a steeper angle of attack.

1 Play the ball slightly further forward in your stance and relax your grip pressure so that your wrists can hinge freely in the backswing.

2 Hinge your wrists almost as soon as you start your takeaway. Feel as though you are pointing the shaft of the club straight up in the air to create a steeper swing plane than normal.

3 Keep your wrists active through impact, but do not scoop the ball into the air by allowing the palm of the right hand to flip skywards. Hinge your wrists upwards through impact to once more set the club on a steep plane.

TRAJECTORY EXERCISE 2

low shots

Hitting the ball lower requires less wrist action and a more compact and controlled swing to shallow out the attack into the ball.

1 Play the ball slightly further back in the stance than for a normal full shot and set a little extra weight on your front foot. You can keep your grip pressure the same as normal, or increase it ever so slightly to reduce your wrist action.

2 Make a conscious effort to avoid hingeing your wrists. Restrict your weight transference and be prepared for the fact that your backswing will be slightly shorter than normal.

3 Keep your hands ahead of the clubface and ball through impact and into the first few feet of your follow-through.

TRAJECTORY EXERCISE 3

varying the height of the shot

You can vary your wrist action through the ball on normal shots to create a slightly higher or lower ball flight. Watch what happens to the flight of the ball when you allow your wrists to become more lively through impact and what happens when you keep them relatively passive.

To be able to vary the height of a shot is a valuable skill particularly on heavily wooded courses where shots may have to be played over or under the branches of trees. But it can also be a useful asset on a links course, playing the ball low to keep it below the wind, or high to ensure that an approach shot stops on a firm, wind-dried green and does not run off the back of the putting surface into thick rough or gorse. Make sure you maintain your normal swing tempo and balance and don't try to hit the shot too hard.

PITCHING EXERCISE 1

the standard pitch shot

The standard pitch shot, played from anywhere between 30 and 80 yards from the green, is basically an abbreviated version of your full swing with a few amendments to the address position to reduce the distance you hit the ball.

1 Stand a little closer to the ball than for a full shot and open your stance so that your hips and feet aim a little left of your intended target to give yourself more room to swing the club through impact. Narrow your stance to improve your balance.

2 Swing the club away in exactly the same manner as you would for a full shot. Hinge your wrists to set the club on a fairly steep plane. How far you swing your arms back depends on how far you want to hit the ball.

3 Turn your chest towards the target as you swing your arms back down to the ball.

4 Use your upper body to release the club through impact and prevent your wrists from becoming too active – one of the major reasons for inconsistent pitching.

PITCHING EXERCISE 2

make backswing and follow-through the same length

Most pitching problems are the result of a lack of tempo caused either by abbreviating the length of the backswing too severely or decelerating the clubhead through impact.

1 Set up as you would to play a normal pitch shot.

2 Keep your backswing and follow-through approximately the same length.

3 Maintain an even tempo throughout the swing. Do not slow down until you have finished hitting the shot.

1   2   3

PITCHING EXERCISE 3

use hips, chest and shoulders as distance reference points

One of the greatest challenges in pitching is being able to control the distance that you hit the ball.

1 Practise hitting the ball when you swing back to hip height, chest height and shoulder height in the backswing.

2 Write down how far you hit the ball with each swing and remember this for when you are next on the course.

PITCHING EXERCISE 4

set your wrists, pump and go!

Most pitching problems are caused by allowing the club to get out of position in the takeaway and the backswing. Use this exercise to feel the correct movement.

1 Set up to play a regular pitch shot of about 50 to 60 yards in length.

2 Make your backswing by swinging your arms away from the ball and hingeing your wrists to set the club on a plane. Stop when you reach this point and experience what the correct position feels like.

3 Pump the club up and down a couple of times to introduce some movement and momentum into your swing and continue with the downswing.

4 Setting yourself in the correct backswing position will give you the confidence to swing freely and confidently through the ball.

1

2

3

4

PITCHING EXERCISE 5

different clubs = extra versatility

You do not have to restrict yourself to pitching with your pitching wedge. Pitching with a 7- or even a 6-iron, allowing the ball to run on landing, is often more effective than using a wedge on a links course.

1 Use clubs with differing amounts of loft to enable you to become a more versatile pitcher.

2 Watch how the trajectory of your shots varies and the amount the ball rolls when it hits the green.

3 Practise hitting pitching shots with anything from an 8-iron to a lob wedge.

PITCHING EXERCISE 6

avoid leaving pitches short

Mental imagery can help you to become more authoritative with your pitching.

Some golf professionals develop such confidence with their chipping that they have the flagstick removed from the hole, as if they were putting.

1 Practise aiming to land the ball on top of the flagstick, rather than on the green. This will automatically lead to a more positive approach to the shot.

2 If your problem is the reverse, aim at the base of the flagstick to become less aggressive through the ball.

CHIPPING EXERCISE 1

the standard chip shot

The standard short-range chip played from just off the green is a relatively simple shot to play, yet many golfers over-complicate the technique by either making too long a swing or by over-using their hands in the shot to get the ball in the air.

1 Narrow your stance at address and play the ball back of centre between your feet. Some players like to set up with their feet open (aiming a little to the left of the target), but it is not essential. Set a little extra weight on your front foot at address. Make sure that your hands are ahead of the ball.

2 Keep your weight on your front foot while swinging your arms away from the ball. Allow your wrists to 'give' a little in response to the momentum of the swing, but remember to avoid consciously hingeing your wrists.

3 Return to your address position at impact. Keep your hands ahead of the ball and your weight on your front foot. Avoid scooping the ball into the air with your wrists, as this leads to all kinds of inconsistent strikes.

CHIPPING EXERCISE 2

how to choke down on the grip

Most golfers understand that they should hold the club further down the grip for extra control on short shots, but very few do it correctly. The most common mistake is to take your normal address position and then simply bend further forwards to reach down the grip, which normally leads to a cramped and slouched set-up.

1 Let the club sit naturally on the ground.

2 Slide the clubhead towards your feet so that the shaft of the club becomes more upright and recreates a similar angle to that of your putter.

3 Tilt forwards from your hips to lower your hands down the grip. Now you can use an elongated version of your putting stroke to play the shot.

CHIPPING EXERCISE 3

create a steeper angle of attack

A downward strike into the ball is fundamental to successful chipping.

1 Place a club six inches behind the ball at address and then hit some practice chip shots.

2 Make sure that the clubhead does not touch the shaft on the ground before striking the ball. This will improve your consistency of strike and also prevent you from trying to 'scoop' the ball into the air with your hands.

CHIPPING FEEL EXERCISE 1

the ladder drill

Where possible, it is advisable to land a chip shot on the green where the bounce is more predictable than in the longer fringe grass. Therefore, one of the key skills in chipping is being able to pick out your landing area and then hit it successfully. Perform this ladder exercise to help you judge the distance you carry the ball through the air with a selection of different clubs.

Use a selection of different clubs so that you get accustomed to the difference in carry/roll between your 6-iron, say, and your sand wedge.

1 Starting at a point just a few feet onto the green, lay five or six shafts on the ground so that they form a ladder. A hole is not necessary, since you are only learning how to carry the ball through the air. The gap between the shafts should be about three feet in length.

2 Standing to the side of the ladder, aim to land the ball in the gap between the first two shafts, then the next one until you can land the ball in each gap with the same club.

CHIPPING FEEL EXERCISE 2

the 'chip and putt for real' drill

A common error that golfers of all levels make when practising the short game is to hit too many meaningless shots. The secret to successful practice is to replicate what might happen on the course as closely as possible, and you should reflect this when you practise.

1 Recreate the pressure of having to get up and down to save par by chipping just one ball onto the green at a time. This will force you to concentrate on every shot and give you a much clearer idea of how good you really are.

2 Always walk onto the practice green and hole out after every chip shot. A good short game is a combination of touch around the greens and the ability to hole the putt. This exercise trains both parts, whereas simply hitting lots of chip shots neglects the important putting aspect.

CHIPPING FEEL EXERCISE 3

different clubs and addresses

Due to the almost infinite number of situations you can find yourself in around the green, no two chip shots are ever exactly the same. Make sure also to practise chipping from upslopes, downslopes, sidehill lies and different lengths and types of grass, and don't forget bare lies.

1 To inject versatility into your technique, you must experiment.

2 Try different clubs, ball positions, lengths of swings and releases to see how the ball reacts off the clubface.

BUNKER PLAY ADDRESS ROUTINE 1

open the clubface before you grip the club

To ensure that the clubface remains open through impact it is vital that you open the face before you form your grip, otherwise it will simply return to a square position through the hitting area and dig too deeply into the sand.

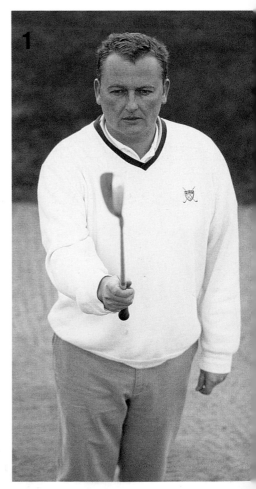

1 Hold your sand wedge out in front of you with just your right hand so that the clubface is in a square position.

3 Place your left hand carefully in position and then re-apply your right hand to complete your grip.

2 Twist the grip to the right through your fingers so that the clubface opens.

BUNKER PLAY ADDRESS ROUTINE 2

the correct address position

Most golfers understand that they need to open their stance a little to play bunker shots, but they are unsure of by how much they should do so. Many make the mistake of simply aiming their feet to the left of the target without making any adjustment for the change in ball position that this amendment to the set-up causes.

1 Stand in the practice bunker and adopt your normal address position with the ball in the centre of your stance.

2 Open your stance by aiming your feet and body to the left of your intended target, but only by a few degrees. Notice how the ball has now moved back in your stance in relation to the line of your feet.

3 Shuffle your feet a couple of inches to the right in the sand so that the ball moves back to its original position in the centre of your stance in relation to the line of your feet. Now you are in the correct address position.

1   **2**   **3**

BUNKER PLAY ADDRESS ROUTINE 3

draw a 'V' shape in the sand

To help you understand how to stand to the ball at address, practise with a 'V' shape drawn in the sand. Your clubface aims down one side of the 'V' directly at the hole, while your feet and body are aligned with the other.

Play the ball forward in your stance in relation to the line of your feet. From here, all you need to do is swing the club along the line of your body, ensuring that you hold your body angles, and the ball will pop out on a cushion of sand.

The more open your stance and the clubhead the higher will be the ball's trajectory as it leaves the bunker. While many bunkers on parkland courses are little more than eye-candy and you could almost putt out of them, the traditional bunkers found on ancient links courses can be seriously deep and steeply faced. Occasionally even the professionals have to admit defeat and play out sideways or even backwards. Once you are confident with your bunker play remember to practise from awkward lies, just below the face or where the backswing is hampered by the rear lip, from steeply raked sand and from compacted, damp sand.

BUNKER PLAY EXERCISE 1

playing the splash shot

Once you have made the adjustments to your set-up, playing the bunker shot is relatively straightforward.

1 Set up aiming several degrees left of your intended target with your feet and body. The further left you aim, the higher the ball will travel at the expense of distance. Shuffle your feet into the sand for a firm footing.

2 Swing back along the line of your feet and body, NOT along the ball/target line. Commit to swinging back to shoulder height for a regular greenside bunker shot.

3 Swing the club back down on the same path as it went up – along the line of the feet and body. Keep your height in the downswing and avoid straightening your legs or dipping into the ball.

4 Your follow-through should be at least as long as your backswing. If you do not swing through to virtually a full finish then you have not accelerated the clubhead enough.

BUNKER PLAY EXERCISE 2

make a one-handed swing

The two main causes of inconsistent bunker play are not making a long enough backswing and failing to utilize the bounce on the sole of the sand wedge through impact.

1 Open the face of your sand wedge by rotating the grip to the right. Once you have done this, grip the club with just your right hand. Make some practice swings while holding the club with just your right hand, ensuring that you swing back to at least shoulder height.

2 In the downswing, splash the clubhead confidently into the sand, making sure that the clubface remains in an open position through impact.

3 Aim to swing through into a virtually full finish. You will only be able to achieve this if your swing is authoritative and the clubface remains open through impact, allowing the bounce angle on the sole of the club to prevent the clubhead from digging into the sand.

PUTTING ADDRESS ROUTINE

recommended pre-putt routine

Although there are no set rules when it comes to putting, it pays to be as orthodox as possible for ultimate consistency. This means adopting a good posture and alignment.

1 Start by placing the putter behind the ball so that it aims directly at your intended line. Make sure that your left foot does not step ahead of the ball as you do this.

2 Tilt forwards from your hips to form your grip on the club so that you adopt a good posture where your arms hang naturally and comfortably from your shoulders. Ideally, your arms should be slightly bent at the elbows to promote the pendulum-style motion that is required in the stroke.

3 Although it is not essential, try to position your eyes directly over the ball so that you get a more accurate perspective of the ball/target line.

1   2   3

PUTTING STROKE ROUTINE

keep head and lower body still

As with the chip shot, the putting stroke is a very simple movement that is often over-complicated by amateurs who fail to adhere to just a couple of basic fundamentals.

1 At address, the ball should be forward of centre in your stance and your hands should be directly above the ball. This gives you the best chance of striking the ball slightly on the upswing to create topspin.

2 As you make your stroke by swinging the putter away with your arms and shoulders, keep your lower body and your head as still as possible so that the putter can track back and through on the correct path. Keep the putter head as low to the ground as possible throughout the backswing.

3 In the downswing, resist the temptation to look up too early to see where the ball has gone and instead focus on swinging the putter through the ball at the same tempo as the backswing. Your backswing and follow-through should be approximately the same length.

PUTTING POSTURE EXERCISE

test your eye-line

It is advisable to set up with your eyes as close as possible and directly above the ball in order to give yourself the best view of the line of the putt. To check your set-up, hold the end of your putter to your nose and see if it covers the ball at address. Similarly, to ensure that the ball is played just ahead of centre in your stance, hang a club from your sternum. The ball should be positioned an inch or so ahead of the shaft towards your front foot.

While it would seem obvious that having the eyes set up directly above the ball should remove some of the errors in putting, one only has to observe a field of professionals during a golf tournament to realize that not all top professionals adopt the most natural of stances – far from it! They utilize a variety of stances, grips, lengths of putter shaft, designs of putter heads and a bewildering assortment of putting actions, but what they are seeking to achieve is a consistent motion which brings the clubhead back to the ball squarely and reliably. Watch the very best putters, however, and they all share a simplicity of action and smoothness of stroke.

PUTTING TECHNIQUE EXERCISE 1

putt with club underneath arms

In the ideal putting stroke your arms and shoulders work together to control the movement of the putter with a pendulum-style motion back and through. Problems occur in the putting stroke when the arms and shoulders fail to work together. This is an exercise to combat this.

1 Place a shaft underneath your arms and across your chest and rock your shoulders gently up and down.

2 Make sure that the whole of your upper body moves together and your arms remain linked to your chest throughout the backswing.

3 Keep your body moving in the same way throughout the follow-through.

READING GREENS EXERCISE

your recommended three-point plan

The top players often take forever to read a putt, and while there is no need to ponder over the line for ages, it pays to be observant and to know what you are looking for. As with the long game, a pre-putt routine is absolutely crucial.

1 Start to read the greens as soon as you walk towards the putting surface after you have struck your approach shot. On the green itself, take your initial look at the putt from behind the ball.

2 Walk to a point midway between the ball and the hole on the low side to get a better perspective of the severity of the gradient and also of the true distance. Look at the length of a putt from more than one angle to avoid being fooled by any foreshortening effects.

3 Walk round the back of the hole if you are still uncertain and back to the other side to view the putt from every angle. This does not have to take too long and can be done in segments as you and your playing partners prepare for your putts.

PUTTING TECHNIQUE EXERCISE 2

the reverse overlap grip

Virtually every professional uses a slightly different grip for putting than for hitting full shots. This is to reduce wrist action during the putting stroke.

1 Form the reverse overlap by holding the club as you would for a full shot.

2 Move your left index finger so that it overlaps the first three fingers on your right hand. Make sure that both thumbs point straight down the grip.

3 Practise this grip constantly to help your hands behave as more of a unit and you will strike your putts more solidly as a result.

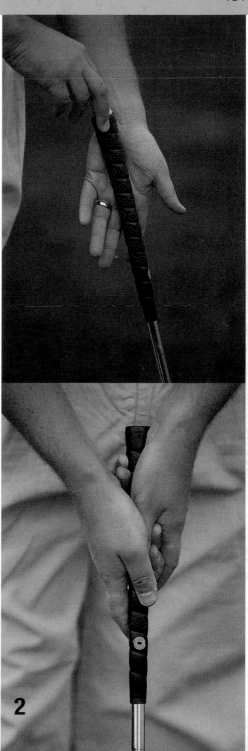

2

PUTTING FEEL EXERCISE 1

judging distance

Good putting is a combination of good technique and good judgement of line and distance. Most players three-putt because they leave their initial approach putt well short of the hole. Unfortunately, there is no substitute for plenty of play and practice to develop your feel, but these exercises will help you to accelerate the learning process.

1 Place a club 18 inches behind the hole on the practice green.

2 Make sure that you follow your pre-shot routine and then hit each ball towards the target of the hole and club.

3 Practise getting each ball into the zone between the hole and the shaft on the ground. This exercise is only complete when you can hit ten balls in a row into the zone behind the hole.

PUTTING FEEL EXERCISE 2

keep the tempo the same

Leaving the ball short of the hole is often due to a lack of rhythm in the stroke. On short putts the stroke is often quick and jerky, while on longer putts the backswing is often greater than the follow-through, leading to a deceleration of the clubhead through impact. Keep the rhythm or tempo of your stroke the same regardless of the length of the putt. All that changes is the length of the backswing and follow-through as they match the length of their stroke to the putt.

1 On a short-range putt, keep the tempo smooth and rhythmical, even though the stroke itself may be fairly short.

2 Your backswing and follow-through should be roughly the same length to keep your tempo consistent.

3 On a longer putt, increase the length of the stroke either side of the ball so that you hit it further. Do not change the tempo as you do not need to hit the ball harder.

4 Increase the length of the stroke to increase the speed at which the putter strikes the ball to make it travel further.

PUTTING FEEL EXERCISE 3

change targets to improve feel

Quickly improve your feel for distance by constantly putting to different length targets. Hit one long putt followed by a medium-length putt followed by a short putt. Changing the length of your stroke helps develop your touch and feel for distance.

It is also important to practise uphill, downhill and cross-hill putts on a regular basis. However, many practice putting greens are often quite level, so you may have to make time to practise on a sloping green on the course itself during a quiet period, perhaps in the evening. But remember that practice on the course is forbidden before a round or play-off on any day of a stroke play competition (Rules of Golf 7-1b). On the other hand, a player may practise on the competition course before a round in match play. Do not practice putting before a competition if the practise putting green is not maintained at the same speed as the greens on the course itself.

SHORT PUTTS EXERCISE 1

keep the face square to the line

One of the keys to consistently holing out from short range is to keep the putter moving straight back and straight through along the line you want the ball to roll. If you are used to allowing the putter to move inside the line in the backswing, the straight-back-and-through stroke will initially feel awkward, but the extra accuracy that you will achieve by keeping the putter face square to the line will help you hole out more convincingly.

1 Find a straight putt of about three feet on the practice green and place a couple of clubs on the ground just over a putter-width apart and aiming straight at the hole.

2 Hit some practice putts, ensuring that the putter head remains within the confines of the shafts. On the backswing, focus on keeping the putter face square to your intended line. In the follow-through, the putter should remain within the shafts and you should focus on keeping the putter face aiming squarely at the hole.

SHORT PUTTS EXERCISE 2

increasing your confidence

If you keep missing short putts, it is very easy to lose confidence. This exercise will help you to prevent this from happening.

1 Drop a ball about three feet away from the hole and ask a friend to hold another club near the ground and make sure that they aim it directly at the centre of the hole.

2 As your friend holds the club in place, make your stroke – ensuring that the shaft of your putter rests on top of the other club.

3 Track the putter back and through along the shaft of the other club and see how easily you can hole the putt now.

SHORT PUTTS EXERCISE 3

how to shorten your backswing

One of the main causes of decelerating the putter through the ball is taking too long a backswing. Top golfers make their backstroke a little shorter than their follow-through. This leads to an acceleration through the ball and a more positive putt and roll.

1 Place a tee peg about eight inches behind the ball and hit some medium-length putts.

2 Make sure that the putter does not touch the peg on your backstroke.

3 Be more authoritative through impact to get the ball up to the hole.

Once you have improved all of the key technical areas of your game, the one remaining aspect of your golf to focus on is your course management. Sensible strategy, good planning and thinking are as equally important to your game as a competent swing. The ability to navigate your way safely round the golf course while avoiding hazards and resisting the temptation to take on unnecessarily risky shots will enable you to maximize your potential as a golfer. All of the game's top players are master tacticians, and you should make it your goal to be just as accomplished at your own level.

During this section, you will learn the course-management techniques that will help you shave shots off your score towards the end of the 10-week programme – from simple preparation such as arriving at the golf club with enough time to spare for a full warm-up, to a more detailed analysis of the most effective way to tackle a tough par-3 or an imposing par-5. At the same time, you will discover how to protect your score over the early holes, play percentage golf like the world's top golfers and develop strategies to record the best possible score on any kind of hole.

Strategy and management

While improving your technique in all areas of the game will undoubtedly pay dividends in the long run, without doubt the quickest way to improve your scores is to pay more attention to your on-course strategy – more commonly known as course management. Every top golfer is a master tactician and they look to squeeze every last drop of potential out of a round by thinking clearly and constructively about how and why they play each and every shot. Your goal is to be just as prudent and to avoid needlessly frittering away shots through poor thinking or strategy.

Just as a top snooker or pool player will often think several shots in advance, so a top golfer will also plan ahead. At the very top level of the game, good course management means leaving the ball below the hole on quick greens or laying up to your favourite yardage to hit a more accurate approach shot. At amateur level, course management is more often a case of damage limitation.

You will rarely see a top professional attempt to hit long irons or fairway woods out of ankle-high rough or try to steer a ball through a two-foot gap in the trees, yet these are the kind of basic errors that higher handicap golfers make all too regularly.

GOOD COURSE MANAGEMENT STARTS
BEFORE YOU TEE OFF
Smart thinking is not just confined to the golf course. How you prepare for a round before you tee off will have a large bearing on how you play and score. Here are a few pointers

that will enable you to start your round in the best possible frame of mind.

Always arrive at the golf course at least half an hour beforehand so that you can check in at the pro shop, get changed and warm-up for your round at a leisurely pace.

Ask staff at the club how the course is playing. The assistant pros will generally be more than happy to tell you some of the key characteristics of the course and even advise you on how best to play some of the holes.

Use your pre-round time to prepare yourself mentally. Remain calm and make sure that you have everything you need to

temptation to make technical changes before you tee off and use your pre-round time on the range as an opportunity to loosen your muscles, hit a few shots with each club and to see what type of shots your swing is producing.

Try the following routine: start by hitting a few pitching wedge and sand wedge shots to give yourself some confidence and then work up through the bag, hitting a couple of shots with each club until you reach the driver.

Before you head to the first tee, always finish your warm-up routine by winding down with your wedges again to restore your smooth tempo.

By this time you should be aware of how well you are swinging and what shape of shot you are hitting most. Accept that this is going to be your shape of shot for the day and allow for it on the course.

play the first hole, such as your ball, tees, scorecard, pencil, glove and pitchmark repairer, readily to hand. The last thing you want to be doing while standing on the first tee waiting to play is rummaging around in your bag trying to find a ball or a tee.

USE THE RANGE TO FIND YOUR SWING FOR THE DAY

The practice range on the day of a golfing competition, or even before a social round of golf, is not the time or the place to work on your swing – that is best left to your practice sessions away from the course. Resist the

PRACTISE A FEW LONG-RANGE PUTTS BEFORE YOU HEAD TO THE FIRST TEE

On the first few holes of a round, it is highly likely that your first few putts on the greens will be from fairly long range. With this in mind, it makes sense to hit at least half a dozen or so 30- to 40-foot putts on the practice putting green before you head to the first tee.

This will enable you to get a feel for the pace of the greens and it will also give you an idea of the length of stroke you will need on the longer putts. It will also help you establish a rhythm for your putting, making a smooth and even stroke.

YOUR RECOMMENDED PRE-ROUND ROUTINE

1 Arrive at the course at least half an hour before you play

Amateurs are notorious for arriving at the golf club with just seconds to spare before they are due to tee off. Leave your house in plenty of time to take a leisurely drive to the golf course. Many professionals like to listen to relaxing music as they drive to the course to put them in the correct frame of mind. You can also use this time to visualize yourself hitting a good opening tee shot and playing the round in exactly the way you would wish.

2 Check in first, then get changed

Always check in at the pro shop before you get changed or do anything else. That way you can then concentrate solely on your preparation and do not have to worry about

returning to the shop or getting caught in a queue before you head to the first tee.

3 Organize the contents of your golf bag

Make sure that you have everything you need to play the opening hole so that you do not have to waste time and nervous energy looking for things when you should be focusing on the tee shot.

4 Spend ten minutes warming up on the range

Loosen up your muscles starting with some gentle wedges and gradually increasing the tempo of your swing until you reach the driver. Do not tamper with your technique.

5 Spend five minutes working on your putting rhythm

Just as the range is not the time to rebuild your swing, the putting green is not the time to work on the mechanics of your stroke. Focus on your rhythm and on rolling the ball smoothly. Hit a few long-range putts and finish by holing several two-footers.

6 Compose yourself before you head to the first tee

Take a few moments to compose yourself and gather your thoughts before you head to the first tee. Slow down your routine and do not allow negative thoughts to linger in your head.

HOW TO OVERCOME YOUR FIRST-TEE NERVES

You probably already know from personal experience that more rounds are ruined by dropping a handful of shots in the opening few holes than by any other on-course disaster. This is perfectly understandable, given that the opening tee shot can often be a nerve-racking experience, but while there is no way to guarantee hitting a fantastic opening drive, there are plenty of things you can do to tilt the odds in your favour.

The first thing to remember is that everyone is in the same boat and that no one is immune to nerves – not even Tiger Woods or Nick Faldo. Your goal is to channel those nerves positively so that you use them to your advantage rather than allowing them to turn you into a gibbering wreck. Here is a checklist to help you overcome the first-tee jitters:

❶ Make sure that you have warmed up thoroughly before you head to the first tee so that you are loose and relaxed.

❷ Use your time on the tee to visualize the perfect shot you want to play. Do not allow negative thoughts to settle in your mind.

❸ Slow down your routine to compensate for the fact that you will instinctively speed everything up when you are nervous.

❹ Stick to your pre-shot routine. Going through the same series of pre-rehearsed motions will distance you from your nerves.

❺ Focus on a small target in the distance to give your brain a specific command to follow and to increase your margin for error.

❻ Finally, check your grip pressure before you start your swing. Just as you will speed up your routine if you are nervous, you will also hold the club tighter and the tension will spread through your body. Soften your grip and relax your forearms.

DO NOT GO FOR BROKE ON THE EARLY HOLES

The opening few holes in a round of golf set the tone for the entire day. If you start badly, you immediately put pressure on yourself to make up for the dropped shots and invariably you start playing more aggressively, and you may find yourself hitting shots recklessly.

The opening three or four holes are an opportunity to settle into your round and to take stock of how you are hitting the ball while your muscles loosen up and you sharpen up your hand–eye co-ordination. If you can avoid dropping more than one shot at any hole in the first half an hour of your round, the chances are you will be able to build on your early confidence and improve as the round continues. However, don't let over-confidence cloud your judgement about what shots to play or what risks to take, and remember to maintain your tempo.

THE BASIC PRINCIPLES OF PERCENTAGE PLAY
Percentage play does not sound the most exciting topic of golf discussion, yet it is probably the most important part of the game for amateur golfers. Knowing when to take on the adventurous recovery shots and, even more importantly, when not to succumb to temptation will make a remarkable difference to your scoring.

Colin Montgomerie's philosophy on course management is a simple yet highly effective one. His motto is to make a bogey his worst score on any given hole. That does not necessarily mean that he accepts the idea of dropping a shot any time he finds himself in trouble out on the course – far from it, in fact. What it does mean, however, is that if he hits an errant shot, he will make sure that his next shot does not leave him in an even worse situation. If Monty's drive lands in the trees, for example, and he believes that he cannot reach the green with his next shot, instead of going for the miracle recovery, he will then reassess his strategy for the hole and work out the best way he thinks he will be able to save his par. Normally this will mean playing the ball back onto the fairway and into a position where he has the best possible chance of firing at the flag.

QUICK TIP
SPLIT EACH ROUND INTO SIX MINI-ROUNDS

An excellent way to put poor play behind you and maintain your concentration during a round of golf is to split each round into six sets of three holes and then aim to play each set in a specific number of strokes. This is a tactic that Swedish Ryder Cup player Per-Ulrik Johansson uses in tournaments. His target is to play each set of three holes in 1-under par. That way if he is 2-over par after the first three holes, he has a new task to focus on for the next three holes and can mentally write off his poor start. Likewise, if he birdies the first three holes, instead of thinking to himself that his run of good play must surely soon come to an end, he can stop thinking about what he has already achieved and focus on a new target.

If you are a high handicapper, set a goal of playing each three-hole set in 3-over par. If you are a mid-handicapper, a more realistic goal may be 2-over par for each set. If your handicap is just above the magical ten figure, you may want to set a target of playing three sets in 1-over par and the remaining three in 2-over par.

Make sure, however, that the target is realistic and that once you can achieve it on a regular basis, you raise the bar again and set yourself a new challenge.

LEARNING THE ART OF GOOD SCORING

Golf can be a strange sport in that you often have days where you struggle throughout the round, rarely find the sweet spot with any club and fail to hole a putt of any significant length, yet when you tally up your score at the end you find that you have played a couple of shots below your handicap. Other times your swing will feel perfectly controlled, you can hit the ball solidly, but find that you simply cannot get the ball in the hole and you walk off the 18th green with a poor score that you feel does not justly reflect how well you have played.

Tour pros are masters at turning mediocre rounds into good ones and, at your own level, you have to learn to do the very same thing. While Tiger Woods will often turn a mundane 72 into a more appealing 69, you must be able to turn your rounds of 84 and 85 into 80s and 81s. This skill is known as 'grinding out a score'.

HOW TO PLAN YOUR ROUND

Strategy plays an important role in golf, but its importance is very often overlooked by amateur golfers, who normally pay scant attention to how they should play any given hole when they stand on the tee. At the other end of the scale, almost every top golf professional will have a detailed game plan for every round, and this means that they will know exactly how they will play each hole.

Assuming that you play most of your golf at the same course, you have the perfect opportunity to devise a similar plan of your own for your next round. Start by thinking about how you normally play each hole and ask yourself if there is a better or more sensible way of playing it.

If there is one particular hole, or holes, that consistently causes you problems, analyze whether it is poor strategy that is to blame or simply bad luck. Chances are it is the former

deciding on their club selection and line of play off the tee. In most cases they will work backwards from the green to the tee, starting the mental process by ascertaining where the pin is placed on the green. Then they will work out from which angle they want to approach the green with their approach shot and then they will determine the club they should use from the tee to put them in that position. All the time they will be thinking of trying to stay well clear of any potential hazards. The last part of the plan is deciding exactly where they will tee the ball within the markers.

The whole thought process should not take more than a few seconds, yet it could easily make the difference between a straightforward par and at least one dropped shot.

You should also make use of the stroke index on the card to plan your round and relieve the pressure.

Uppermost in your mind should always be the fact that you do not have to play perfect golf to become a single-figure handicapper. At the nine most difficult holes on the course – those marked one to nine on the scorecard stroke index – you are expected to drop a shot. These are the holes where you should pay most attention to your course management, since while a bogey is an acceptable score, if you can make a par, you then have the luxury of having a stroke in hand over the card, which you may find useful later in the round.

On the stroke index one to nine holes, the safety net of the stroke means you can become a little more aggressive in your approach. You should, however, always temper this enthusiasm.

rather than the latter. If so, adopt a totally different strategy the next time you play, just to break the pattern.

WORK BACKWARDS FROM GREEN TO TEE
WHEN DEVELOPING YOUR STRATEGY
Most top players will look carefully at the shape and characteristics of each hole before

PAR-3 STRATEGIES

Capitalizing on the par-3 holes is one of the keys to keeping a good score ticking over. If you can par all of the par-3 holes during a round, which is well within most golfers' capabilities, you set yourself up for a decent score.

AVOID COMPLACENCY AT ALL COSTS

The most important thing to remember when playing any par-3 hole is to avoid falling into the trap of assuming that you are going to make a par simply because the hole is relatively short.

Complacency is the main cause of dropped shots on par-3 holes. Experienced golfers are aware that par-3 holes often have fairly small greens that are guarded by bunkers, water, rough or slopes and, therefore, they spend

PLANNING AND PLAYING PAR-3s

1 Do not assume you are going to make a par just because the hole is short.

2 Do not be tempted to go for pins tucked behind bunkers or water.

3 Look to see where most of the hazards are situated.

4 Check the bail-out areas on the longer par-3s.

5 If you know you cannot reach the green, do not try.

more time thinking about their club selection and strategy on these holes than on the seemingly more difficult par-4s and par-5s.

ON LONG PAR-3S –
LOOK FOR THE BAIL-OUT AREAS
It is very likely that some of the longer par-3s – especially those that are close to 250 yards long off the back tees – may sometimes be out of reach even for the accomplished player. Course designers are aware of this and they will invariably make provisions for the higher handicapper or shorter hitter by incorporating a bail-out area into the design of the hole. Sometimes these areas are not always immediately obvious to the eye, but if you look carefully, there will usually be an area of land short of the hole where you can safely play into, keeping the ball away from the hazards that surround the green.

This is a situation where it is easy to fall into the trap of succumbing to peer pressure or letting your ego rage out of control by insisting on playing for the green when you know that you cannot make it. A controlled shot into the bail-out area followed by a deft chip will leave you with a good chance of making your par, or a bogey at the very worst. A wild lunge at the ball off the tee with a straight-faced club could land you in big trouble.

ON SHORT PAR-3S – CLUB SELECTION IS THE KEY TO FINDING SMALL GREENS
If you think of some of the most treacherous holes in professional golf, it may come as a surprise to find that many of them are

actually par-3s: the notorious 17th hole at Sawgrass in Florida is only 140 yards long; the 12th hole at Augusta National in the Masters normally plays at around 155 yards; while the Postage Stamp at Troon is a mere 126 yards from tee to green. All of these holes can easily cause problems for golfers because they place a heavy premium on accuracy from the tee.

Short par-3 holes are invariably very well guarded by deep bunkers, water or rough, which means that club selection is of paramount importance. Think very carefully about the strength and direction of the wind and look to see where most of the trouble is located. In most cases, hazards are

QUICK TIP

WHY A BOGEY IS NOT ALWAYS A BAD SCORE ON A PAR-3

One of Colin Montgomerie's favourite expressions is that bogeys add up slowly during a round, but double bogeys add up very quickly indeed. There is nothing more frustrating than making a double bogey five on a par-3 hole. This is bordering on a criminal offence because it is so avoidable and normally caused by compounding an error off the tee with a poor choice of second shot. Here are some pointers to avoid this situation.

1 If you hit a poor tee shot on a par-3 hole make sure that your second shot lands safely on the green.

2 You do not always have to try to knock the ball stone dead to the hole as that often means taking on a risky shot.

3 Get the ball on the green, two-putt and walk off without doing too much damage to your scorecard.

positioned in front of the green, so it is often a good idea to hit an extra club off the tee so that even a mistimed or badly struck shot still has a chance of making it to the green.

PAR-4 STRATEGIES

Par-4 strategies

These holes can range from anywhere between 251 yards and 470 yards in length, so it is obvious that there is no clear-cut strategy that you can apply to each and every par-4 that you come up against.

The key to all par-4 holes is safely negotiating the tee shot. On long par-4s you need to be fairly long and straight to stand a good chance of making par, while on the shorter par-4s, accuracy is the key to setting up a birdie opportunity.

On short par-4s, if length is your strength, go for the green, otherwise play it safe off the tee, leaving a full shot to the green.

There is a popular school of thought that says you should hit a long iron or fairway wood for accuracy instead of a driver on short par-4s. While that may be true some of the time, it is a sweeping statement that can sometimes do your score more harm than good.

The reason why many coaches advocate playing for accuracy off the tee on short par-4s is because holes in the 260- to 320-yard region are often designed to punish those who attempt to drive as close as possible to the green. The fairway is generally very tight and the landing area often narrows as it approaches the green, making it difficult for you to keep the ball in play off the tee, while the putting surface itself is likely to be very small and guarded by bunkers and other hazards.

Another way of looking at the situation, however, is that if length and accuracy off the tee are your best assets, taking out the driver and getting the ball close to the green takes the pressure off your short game and gives you the opportunity to take three more shots to get down and still make a par. And, of course, you have the outside chance of making a birdie with a deft chip or pitch.

However, the above strategy is only worth considering if you are a long hitter. If you are a short or inaccurate driver the gamble is not worth taking, because you will have to swing harder and faster to achieve the required distance – an approach that normally ends in tears. A much smarter option for the less

powerful, or less consistent, golfer is to hit a smooth long iron or fairway wood into the widest part of the fairway and leave a full shot into the green.

ON LONG PAR-4S – GO FOR ACCURACY OVER POWER EVERY TIME

Most of the longer par-4 holes on any golf course are likely to fall into the stroke index one to ten category which means, of course, that you get a shot on most, if not all, of them. Study the card before your round and note where you'll get strokes. The last thing you

PLANNING AND PLAYING PAR-4s

1 Always check the course planner or yardage boards on the tees for information about the hole.

2 Plan your tee shot so that you avoid hitting unnecessarily into fairway hazards.

3 If the hole is short, check to see where it can bite you.

4 On short par-4s play to your strengths – long accurate hitters may want to get as close as possible to the green. Shorter hitters should play more strategically.

5 On a long par-4 with a low stroke index, make your shot count. Play the hole as a par-5 if it relieves the pressure.

6 If you are able to pin high with approach shots this will take the pressure off your short game.

want to be thinking about when standing on the tee of a 450-yard hole is trying to crush your drive as far as possible. If you think the hole is tough before you hit your drive, it will be even more difficult when you have to chip the ball sideways back onto the fairway and then still have 280 yards to go to reach the green.

Statistically, long par-4s are the holes that cause the most damage during a round of golf, so regardless of whether you are a long or short hitter, accuracy off the tee is your priority. For the longer hitters, a smoother swing is likely to lead to better contact with the ball and good distance, while the shorter or more wayward drivers will benefit from keeping the ball in play off the tee and then being able to play their second shot from the fairway instead of the rough or the trees. Remember that a bogey is an acceptable score on a tough par-4.

PAR-5 STRATEGIES

Par-5 strategies

The top professionals usually view par-5s as birdie-opportunity holes where they can expect to pick up at least one shot on the scorecard. They are also good news for amateurs because the extra length of the hole gives you a little margin for error and a chance to recover if you hit a poor drive or a wayward second shot. At the same time, the shorter par-5s give you more of a chance to make a safe and straightforward par as well as the occasional birdie. Together with the par-3s, the manner in which you play the par-5s will influence your score at the end of the round. If you can limit yourself to making no worse than a par at each of the long holes – which is well within your capability – you will be doing just fine.

FIRST THINGS FIRST –
LENGTH AND DIFFICULTY OF HOLE
DETERMINE TEE SHOT STRATEGY
One of the first things you need to appraise when deciding on your approach to any given par-5 hole is your chance of reaching the green or thereabouts in two shots. If you are a long hitter and/or the hole is fairly short and straightforward, then taking a driver off the

tee is a calculated risk that might be worth taking since you may be able to reach the green with your second shot to set up a good birdie opportunity or, at worst, a simple par.

If, however, the hole is a dogleg 550-yard monster, it will play as a genuine three-shotter for all but the most pumped-up professionals. If this is the case, you have several options to consider on the tee. Most golfers think that they have to hit a driver on a long par-5, but that is far from the case. Although a long iron or fairway wood may leave you 30 or 40 yards back down the fairway compared with your driver, you are more likely to find the fairway and since you cannot reach the green in two shots anyway, the extra distance off the tee is not that important. You can make that yardage up with your next two shots instead.

As an experiment, the next time you play a long par-5 resist the temptation to hit the driver off the tee and see how you score on the hole. It is my bet that you will find the hole easier than you think.

IF YOU CANNOT REACH IN TWO, LAY UP TO YOUR FAVOURITE YARDAGE
A common strategy that top players use on par-5s if they know that they cannot reach the green with their second shot, is to purposefully lay up well short of the hole so that they can play their third shot with their favourite club – normally a pitching wedge or a 9-iron. These players know that they can land the ball within ten feet of the pin from 100 yards out with this club, so even though 'laying up' is regarded as a safe play, when you play to your strengths it is actually an attacking option.

The lay-up is also a sensible strategy because it enables you to hit a full shot into the green. Very often when you go for the green with your second shot on a par-5 you mishit the shot and leave yourself an awkward length pitch over bunkers or water where you will need exquisite touch to get the ball close to the hole. From further back, you can comfortably make a confident full swing with your favourite club.

MASTER YOUR GAME FROM WITHIN 70 YARDS TO TAKE CONTROL OF LONG HOLES
In most cases, for the amateur golfer, par-5s will be out of reach in two shots. Therefore your third shot into the green is likely to be from between 40 to 80 yards out. This is the distance where the world's top golfers are so deadly accurate. From this kind of range, a top player will be disappointed if he does not land the ball within seven or eight feet of the hole, or even closer on some of the shorter-length pitch shots.

The quality of your pitching holds the key to unlocking the par-5s. While you do not have to be as accurate as the professionals, it is important that you develop the skill to judge the distance correctly so that you can get your pitch shots onto the putting surface every time. Admittedly, that sounds very simple, but you would be surprised at how many golfers – low handicappers included – often leave pitch shots well short of the putting surface, purely and simply because they do not know what length of swing to make to match the distance of the shot. Consult the course planner, if there is one, and pace out the distance to the front of the green to know precisely how far you are hitting.

If you can get every pitch shot on the putting surface, two-putt and then walk to the next tee, you will notice a dramatic difference in your scores.

PLANNING AND PLAYING PAR-5s

1 As with the par-3s, do not get complacent and assume that you will make a par, particularly on a short par-5 hole.

2 Decide whether you think you can reach, or get close to, the green in two shots.

3 If the hole is reachable in two shots, you can risk hitting the driver.

4 If the hole is too long to reach in two, opt for accuracy over power off the tee.

5 Lay up to your favourite distance to the hole when planning your second shot on a long hole.

6 Do not panic if you find yourself in trouble. Use the extra yardage on the hole and the extra stroke to get your ball safely back in play.

7 Make sure that pitch shots land on the green.

INDEX

ACKNOWLEDGEMENTS

Executive Editor Trevor Davies
Editor Charlotte Wilson
Deputy Art Director Geoff Fennell
Production Manager Ian Paton
Picture Library Manager Jennifer Veall

PICTURE ACKNOWLEDGEMENTS

SPECIAL PHOTOGRAPHY ©**Octopus Publishing Group Limited**/Mark Newcombe.
OTHER PHOTOGRAPHY **Octopus Publishing Group Limited**/Angus Murray 51, 80 left, 108, 111, 141, 142, 148 top.

YOUR STATS

BC *02/09*

☐ HOLE

Fairway hit
☐ YES ☐ NO ☐ NOT APPLICABLE

Green in regulation ☐ YES ☐ NO

Approach shot/tee shot short of green ☐ YES ☐ NO

Chip shot up and down
☐ YES ☐ NO ☐ NOT APPLICABLE

Chip to within five feet and holed putt
☐ YES ☐ NO ☐ NOT APPLICABLE

Chip to within five feet missed putt
☐ YES ☐ NO ☐ NOT APPLICABLE

Sand save in two shots
☐ YES ☐ NO ☐ NOT APPLICABLE

Sand save in three shots
☐ YES ☐ NO ☐ NOT APPLICABLE

Number of total putts
Three putt ☐ YES ☐ NO

Three putt from long range
☐ YES ☐ NO ☐ NOT APPLICABLE

Three putt from short range
☐ YES ☐ NO ☐ NOT APPLICABLE

Approach putt short of hole
☐ YES ☐ NO ☐ NOT APPLICABLE

Putt holed within 10 feet
☐ YES ☐ NO ☐ NOT APPLICABLE

Putt holed 10–20 feet
☐ YES ☐ NO

Putt missed from short range
☐ YES ☐ NO

Pitch shot played
☐ YES ☐ NO

Pitch shot up and down in two
☐ YES ☐ NO ☐ NOT APPLICABLE

Pitch shots up and down in three
☐ YES ☐ NO ☐ NOT APPLICABLE

OVERALL PERFORMANCE

18-hole total:
Fairways hit:
Greens in regulation:
Total putts:
Approach shots short of the green:

Total three-putts:
Total up and downs:
Sand saves:
Pitch shot saves:
Short putts missed:

NOTES AND HIGHLIGHTS OF THE ROUND

OVERALL   HIGHLIGHT OF THE ROUND